SPECIAL RECOMMENDATION FOR PAINTINGS BY YOUNG ARTISTS

JOLIN CHEN

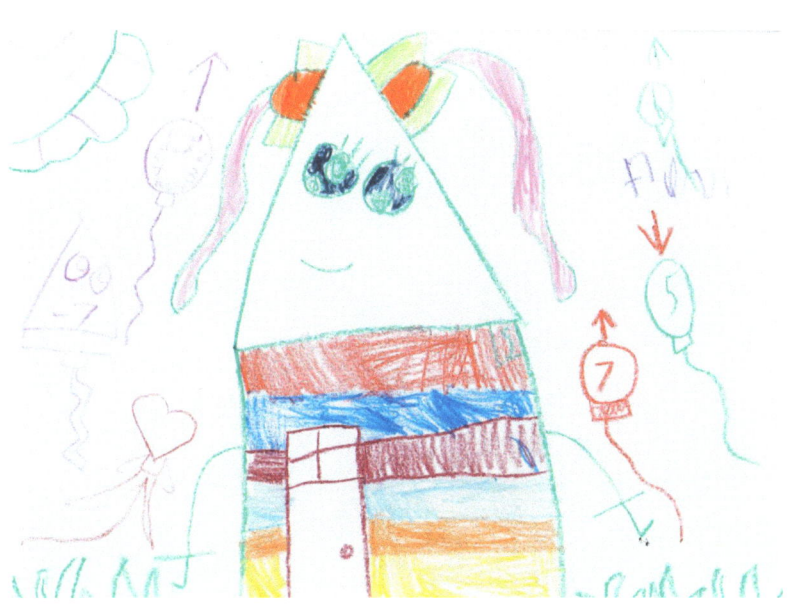

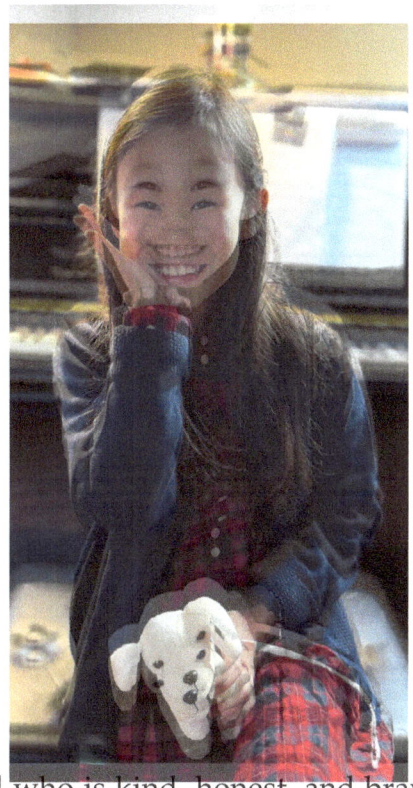

Jolin Chen is an eight-year-old girl who is kind, honest, and brave. Currently, she is a second-grade student who loves drawing, especially color matching. Her favorite hobby is reading; she enjoys comic books, picture books, and graphic novels most.

Jolin's drawing experience started in a summer camp when she was four. She learned how to paint with her fingers and palms and enjoyed drawing on the walls with crayons in her bedroom. Her passion never stopped; she learned to paint with crayons, markers, colored pencils, and acrylics. Her innocent and imaginative color combinations are all expressed in these works.

This collection features Jolin's work starting in 2020. During the pandemic, painting became her source of happiness, and these immature yet childlike works reflect the colorful world in her heart. By 2022, Jolin liked to read biography books. She is fascinated by the experiences of many painters, with Frida Kahlo being the most influential. Accordingly, she gave a brief presentation on Frida Kahlo's biography in first grade. Jolin admires Frida Kahlo's strong personality, fighting spirit, and love for painting.

"Reading thousands of books is not as good as traveling thousands of miles." Jolin's parents enjoy taking her on trips worldwide, hoping she can experience different cultures and appreciate the unique artistic characteristics of each country. During her travels, Jolin visited landmarks such as Sagrada Familia and La Pedrera in Barcelona, Spain, where she saw Gaudí's distinctive architectural style and urban construction with vibrant colors. She also visited the Aegean Sea in Greece, admiring the blue and white buildings along the coastline. In Tokyo, Japan, she witnessed a colorful light show, and at the Palace Museum in Beijing, China, she felt the depth of Chinese culture. Moreover, during her trip to Rome, Italy, Jolin saw the incredible manuscripts of Da Vinci's paintings and other whimsical creations. Jolin's parents hope she maintains an optimistic attitude and draws beautiful moments from life.

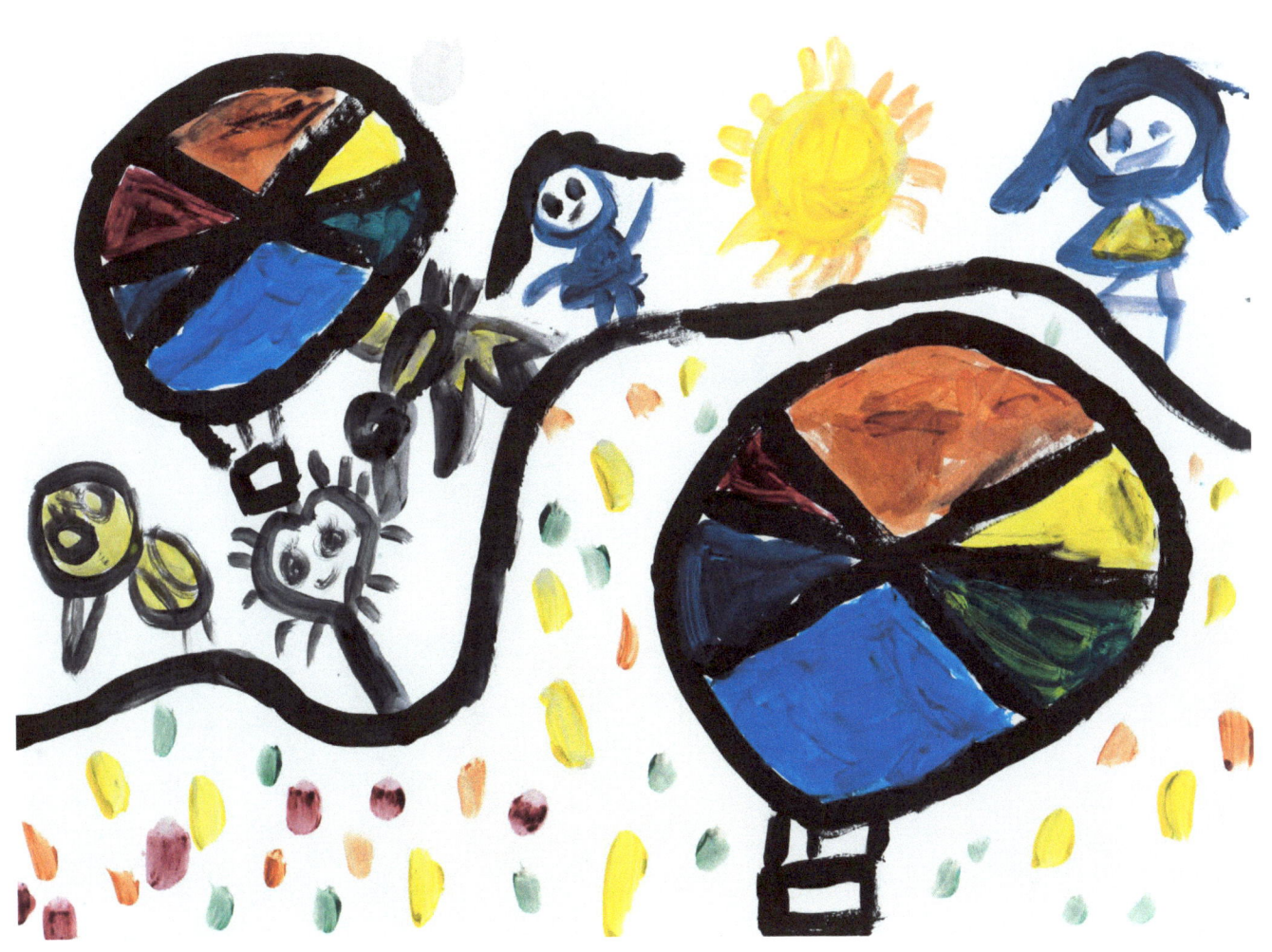

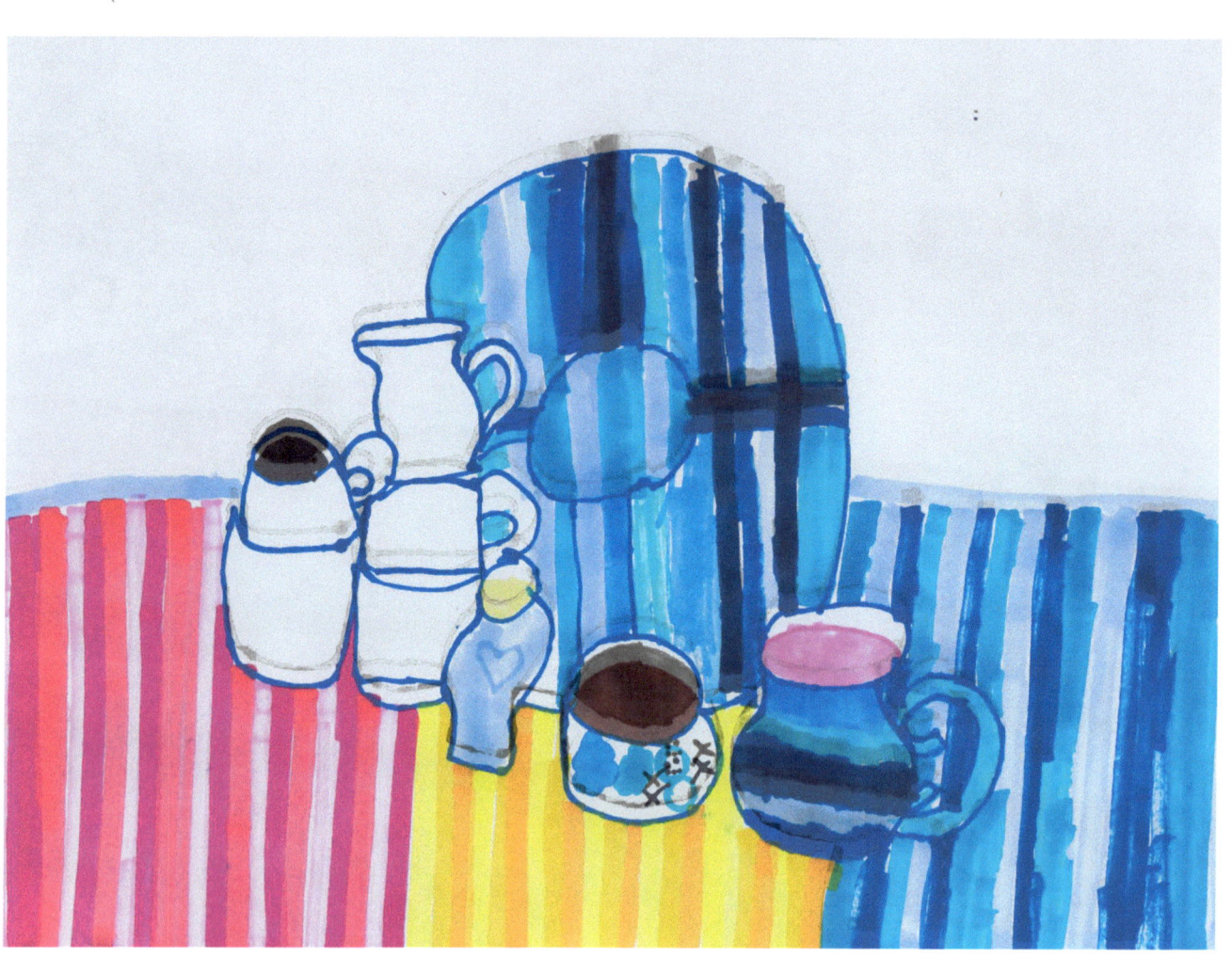

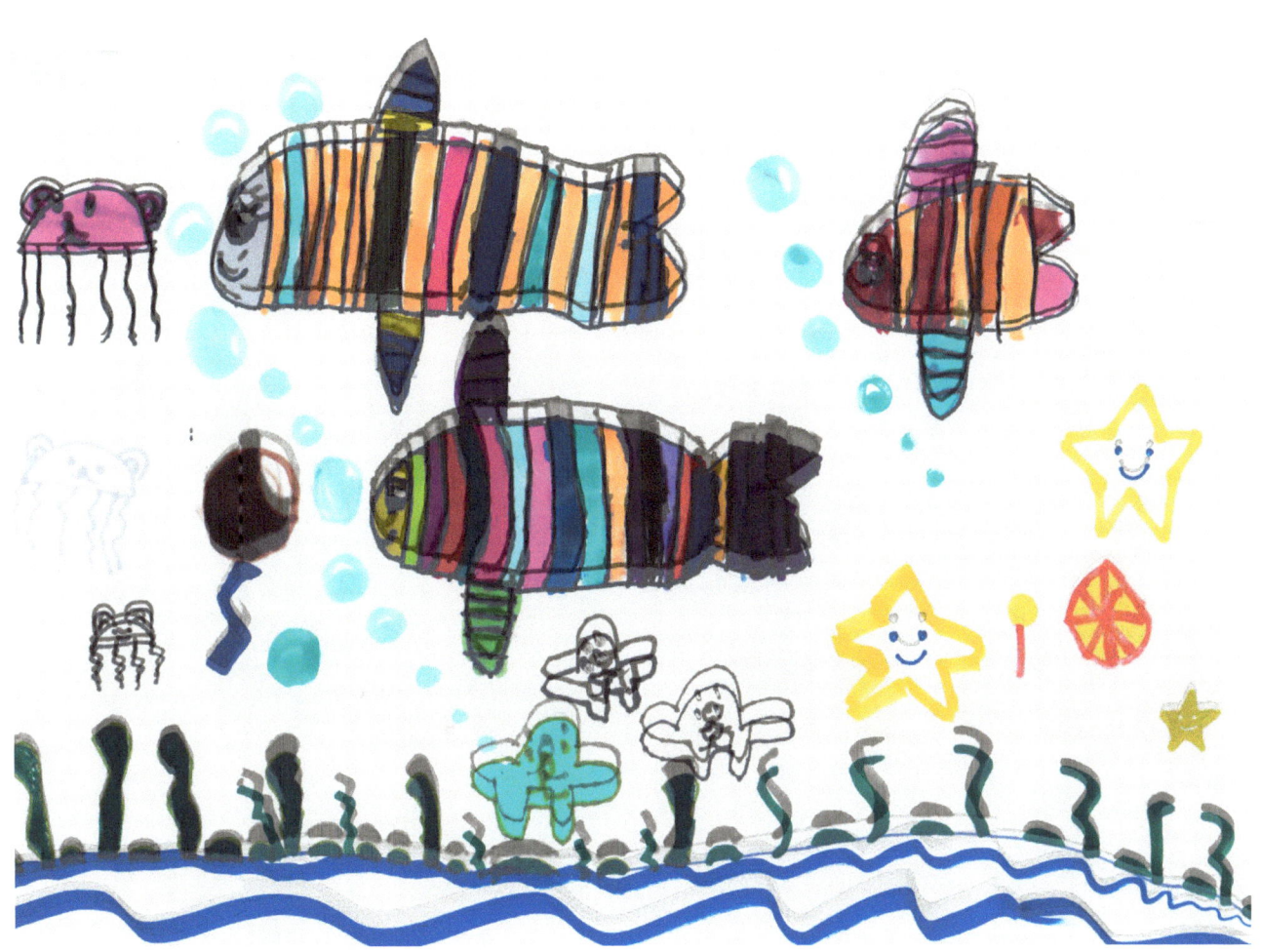

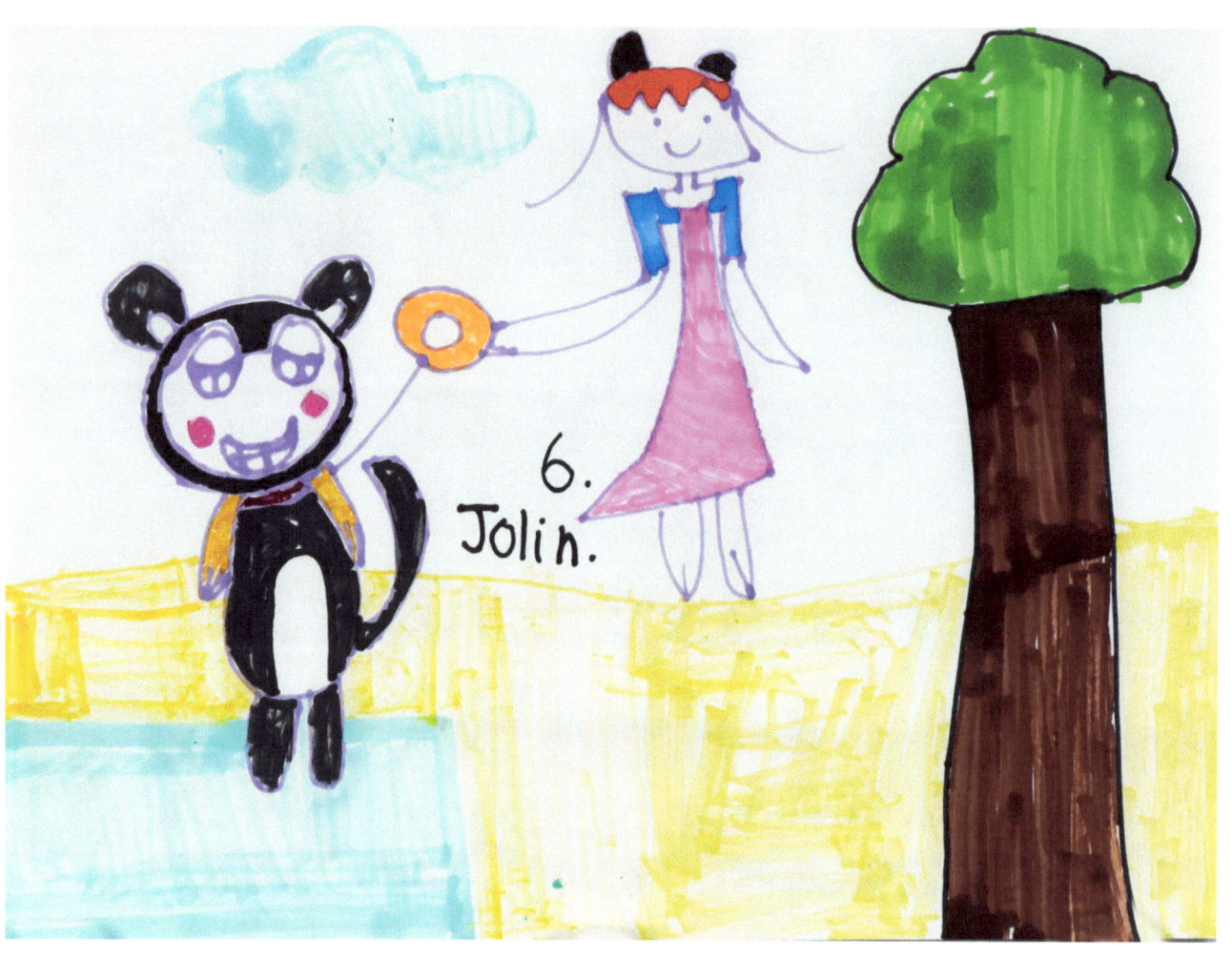

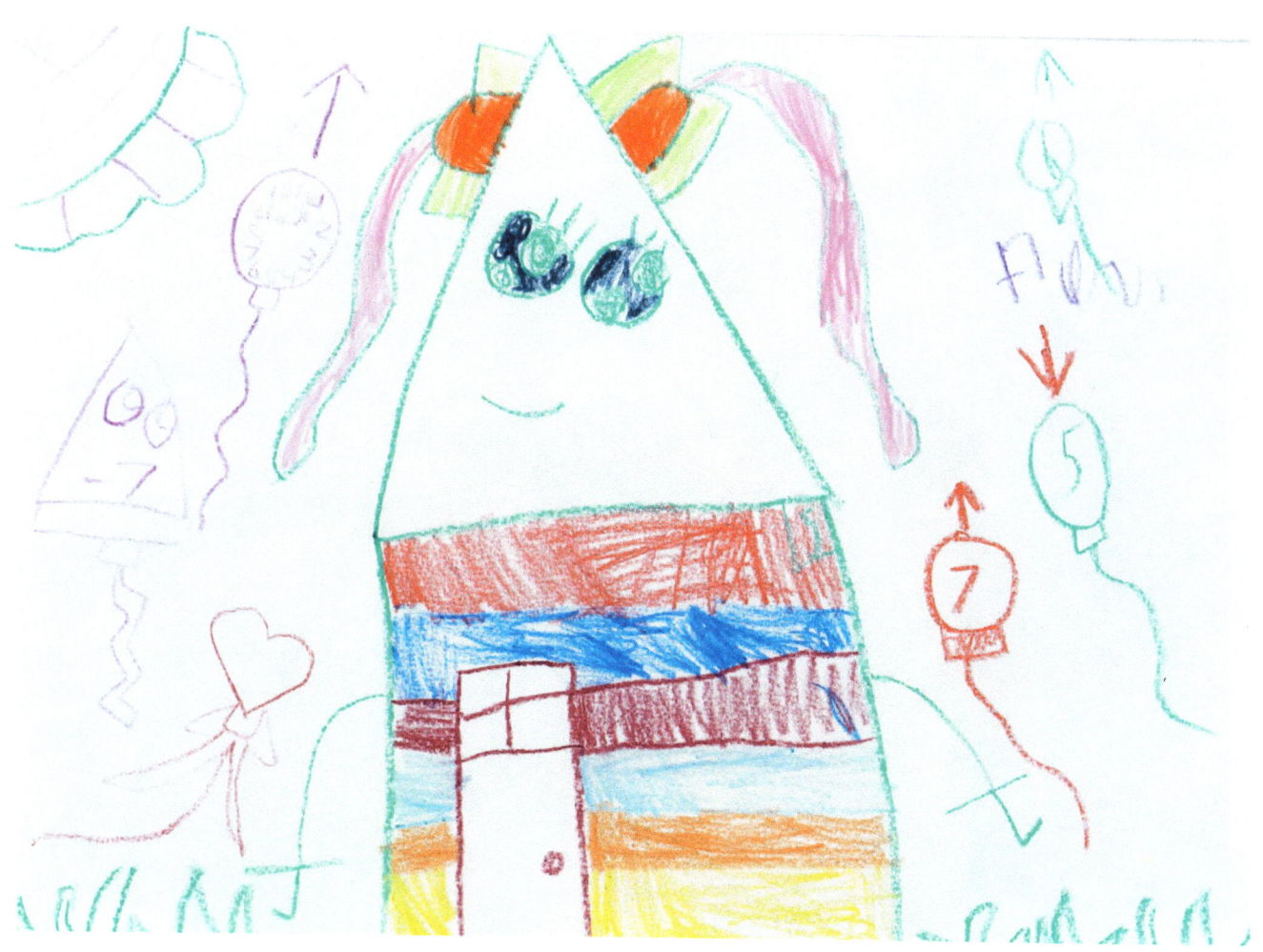

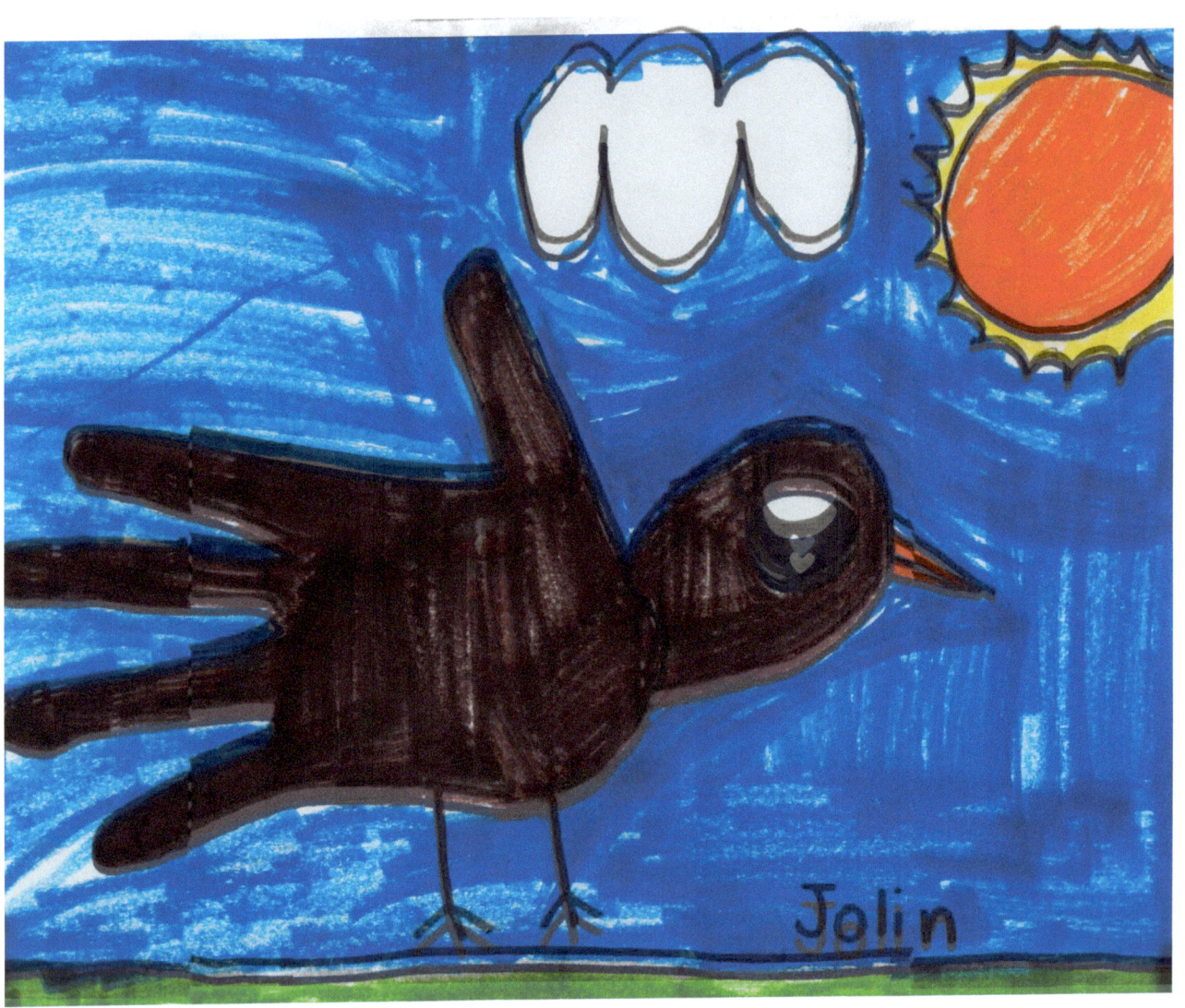

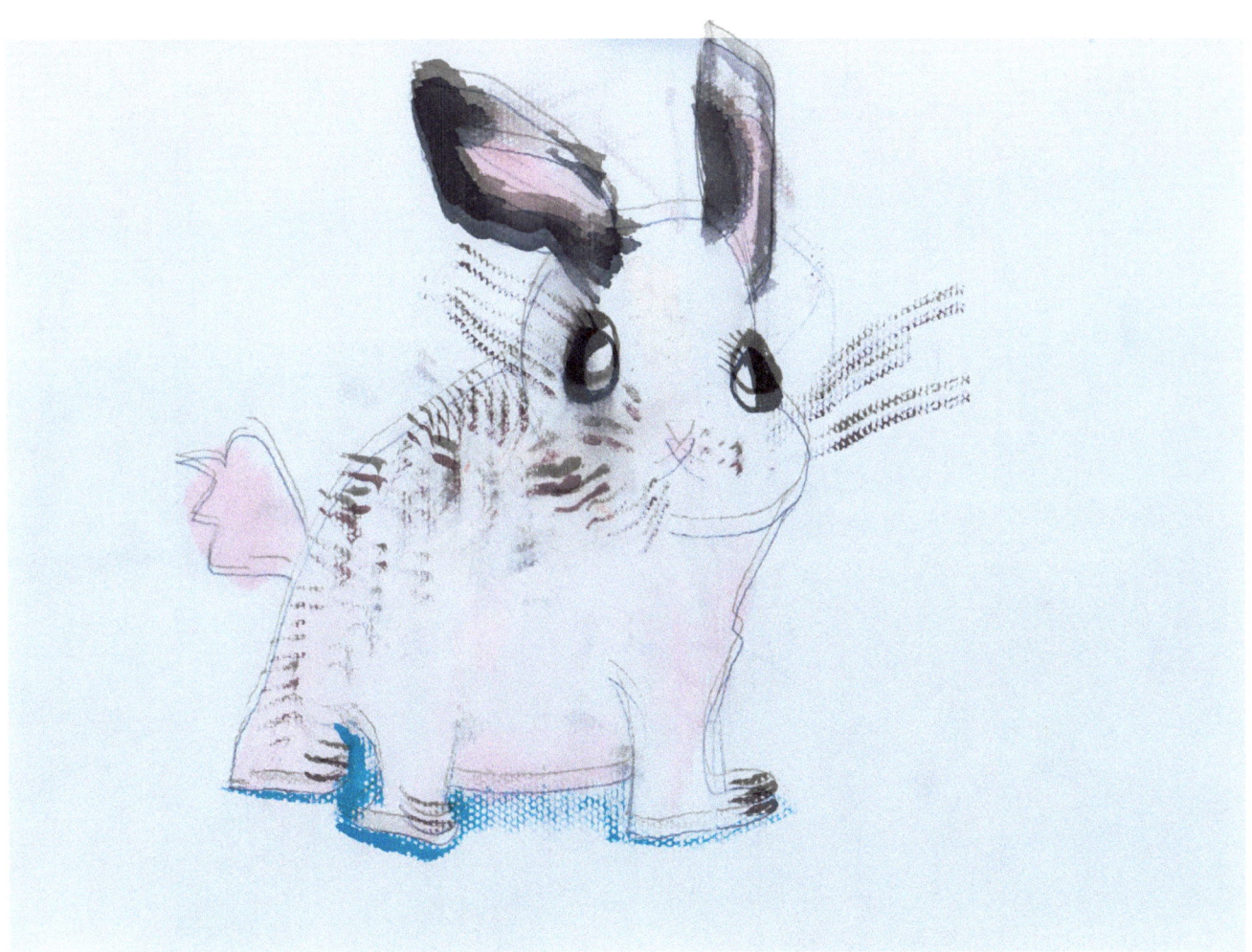

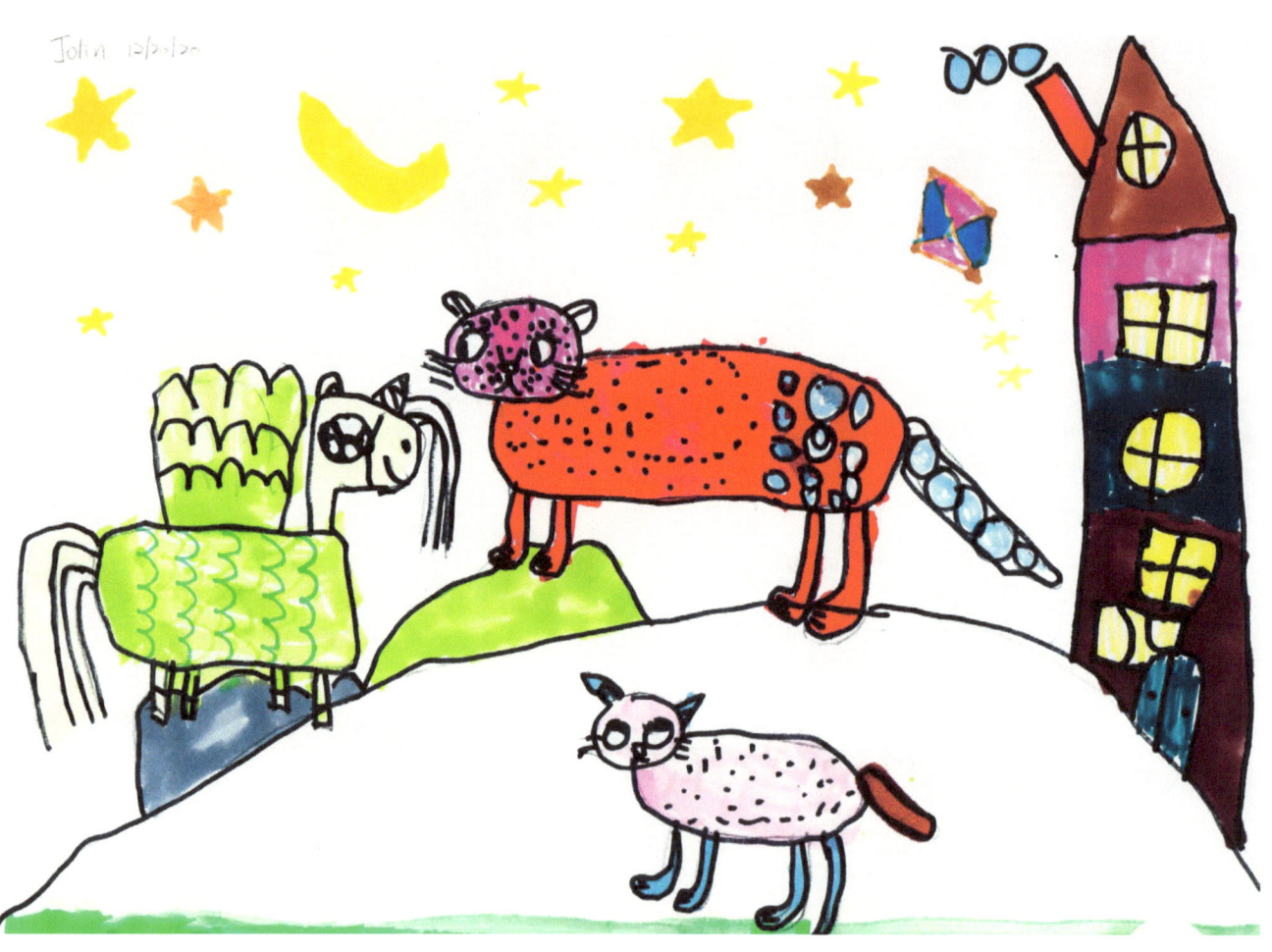

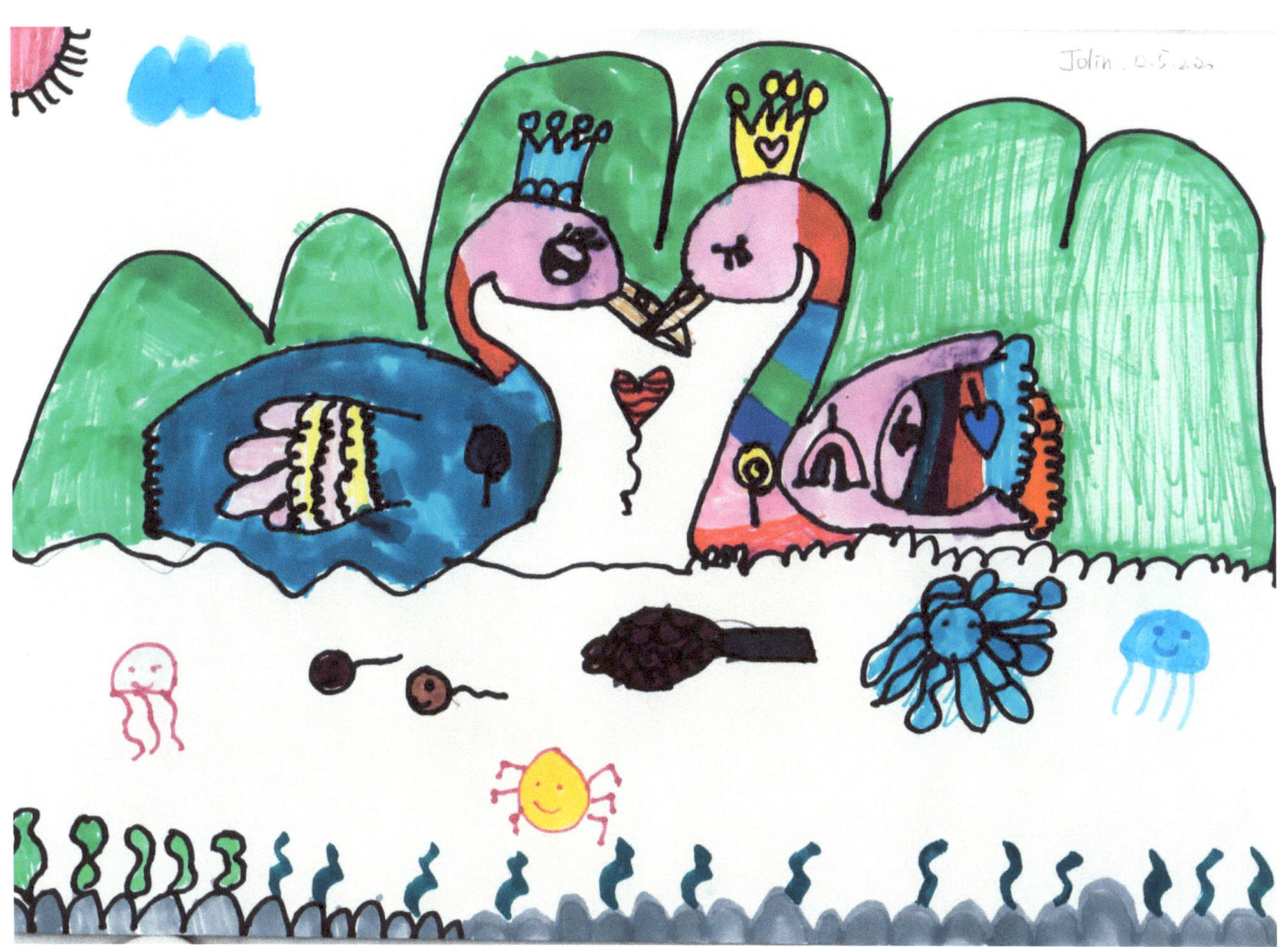

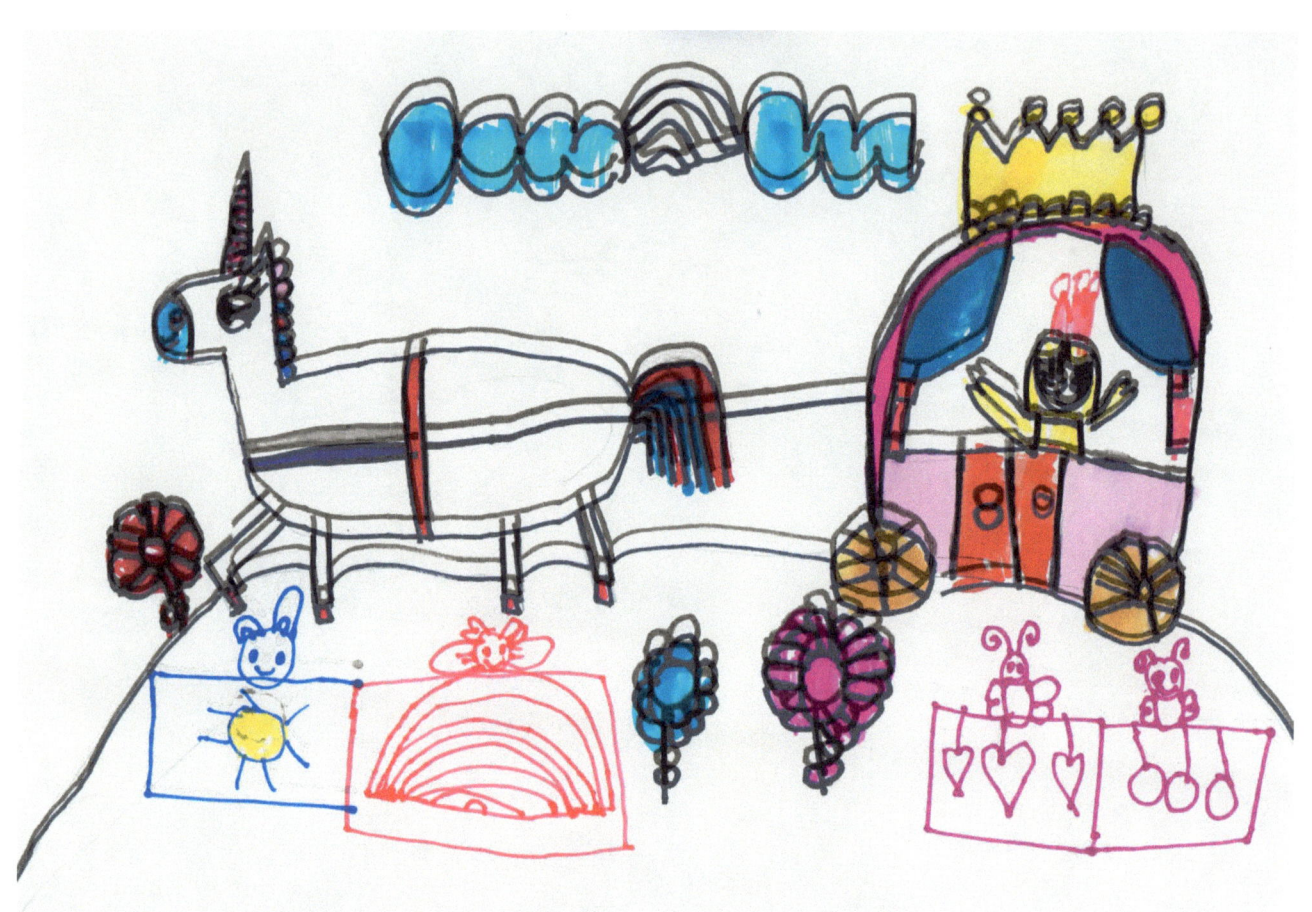

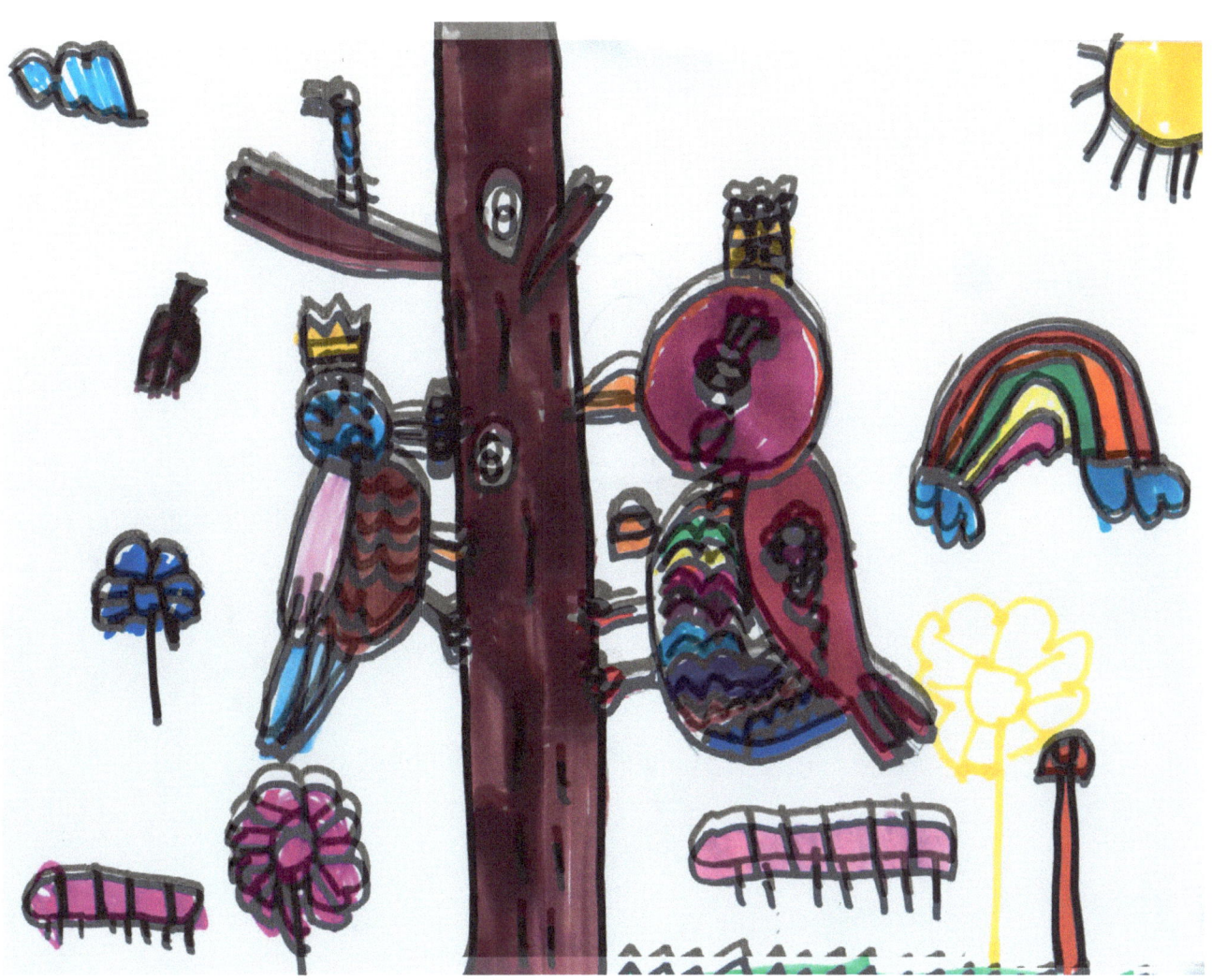

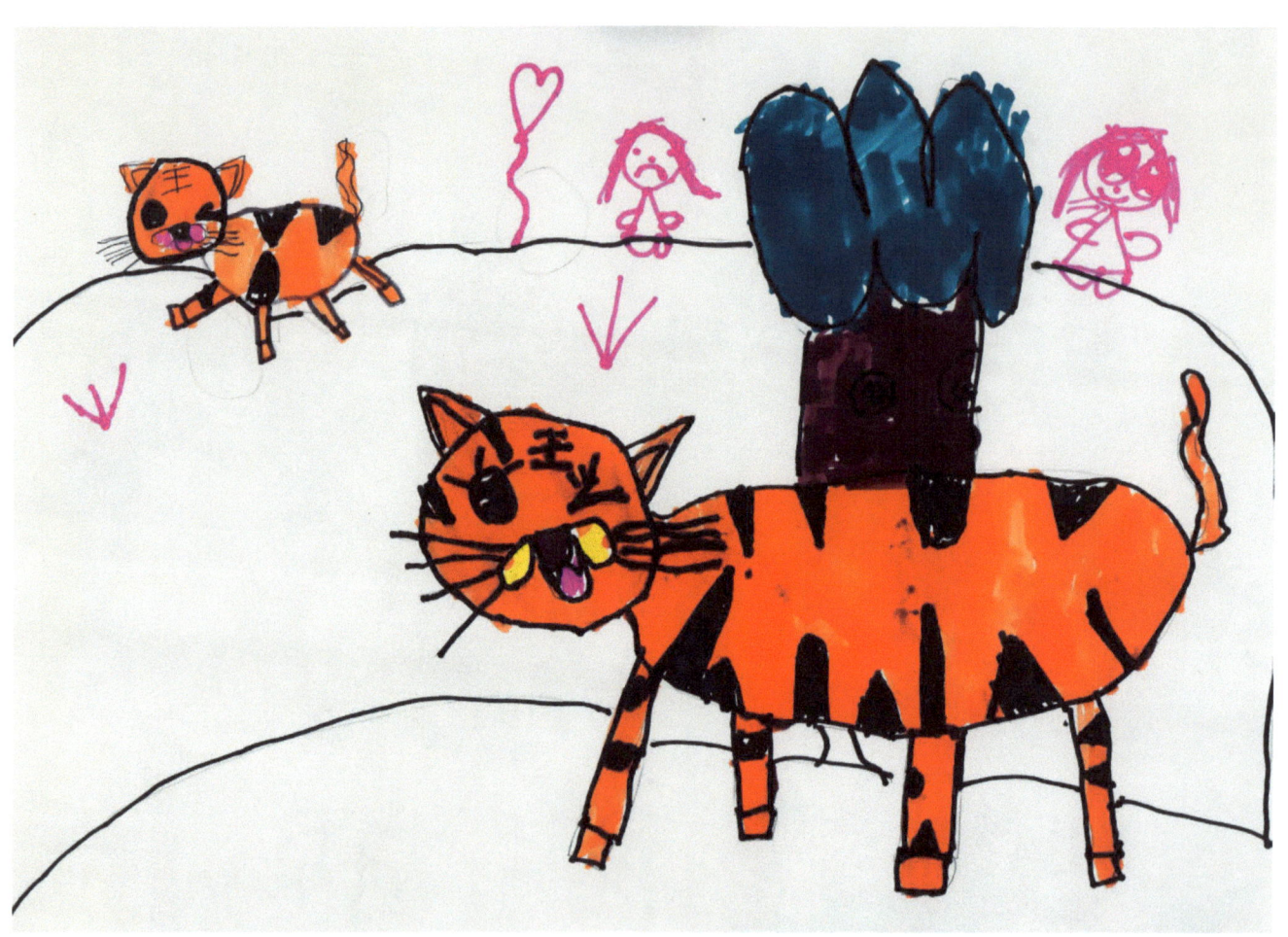

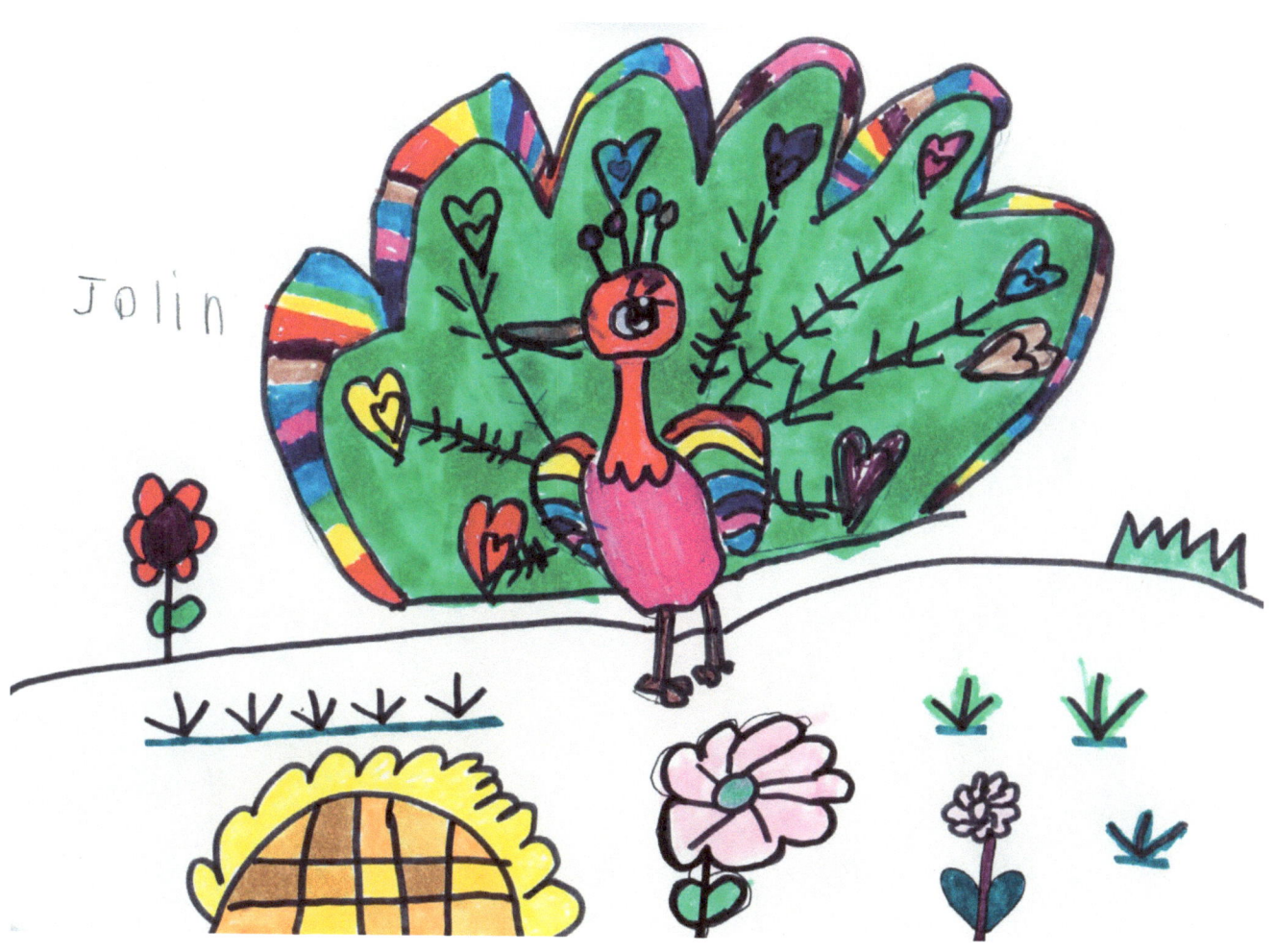

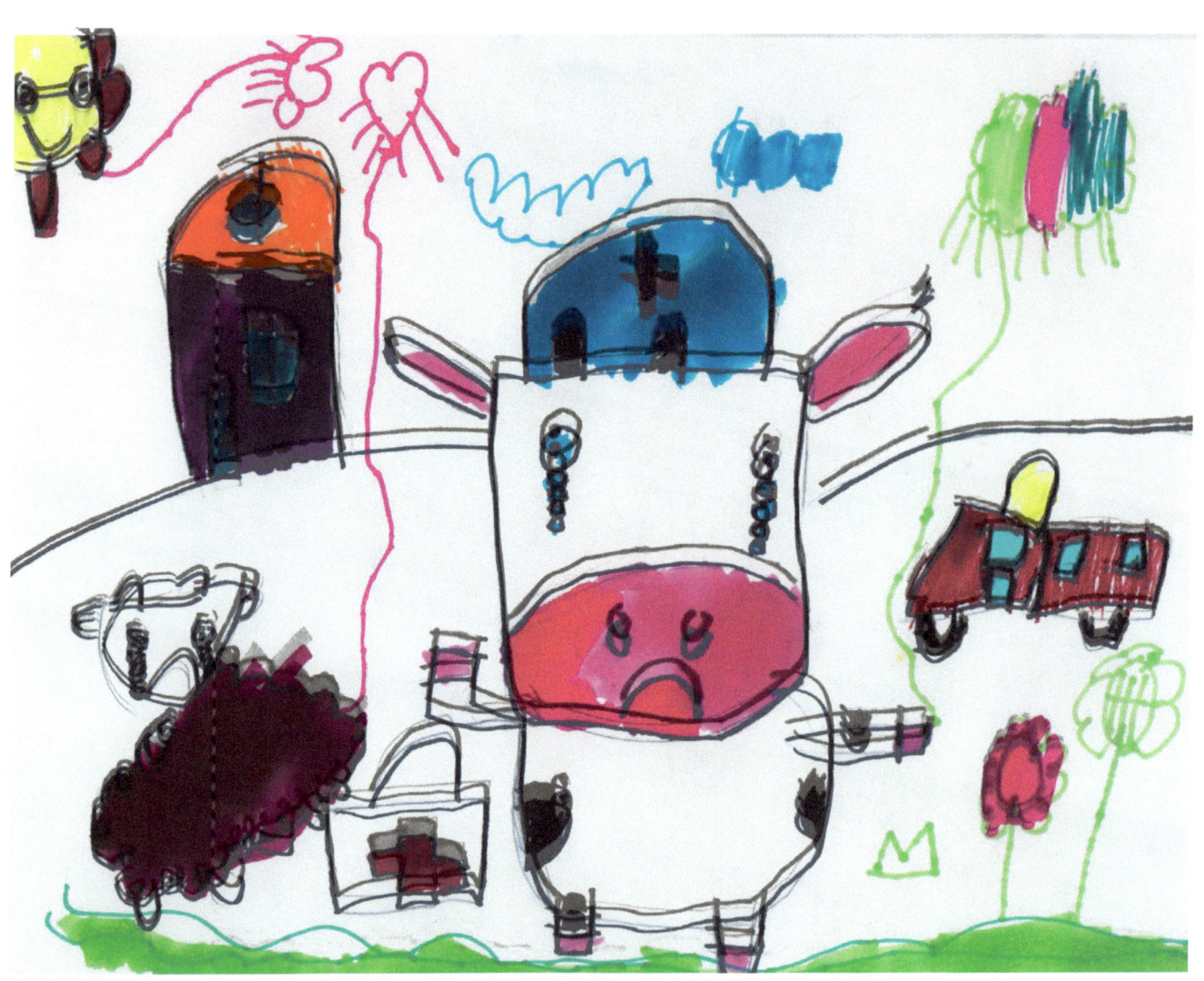

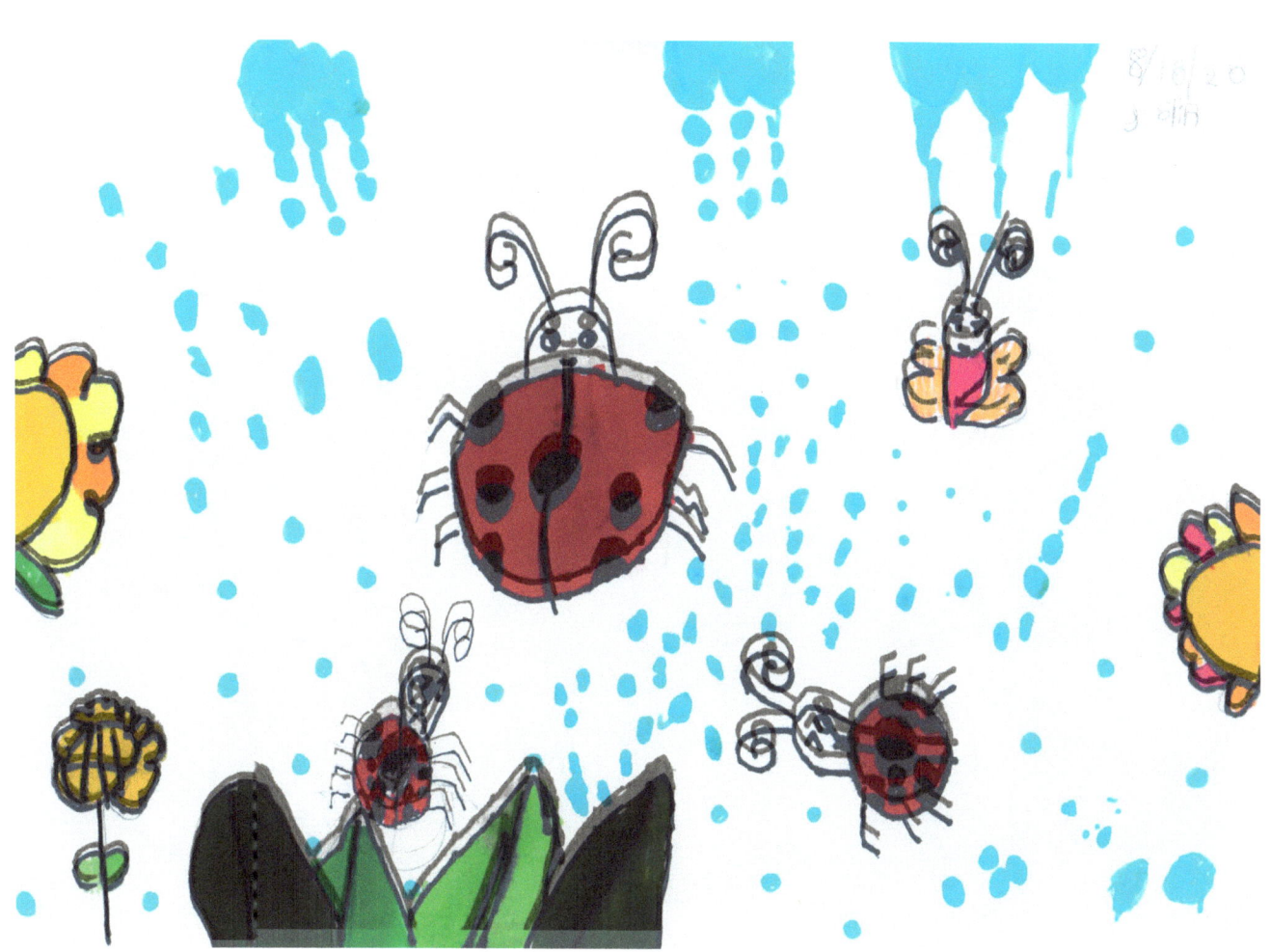

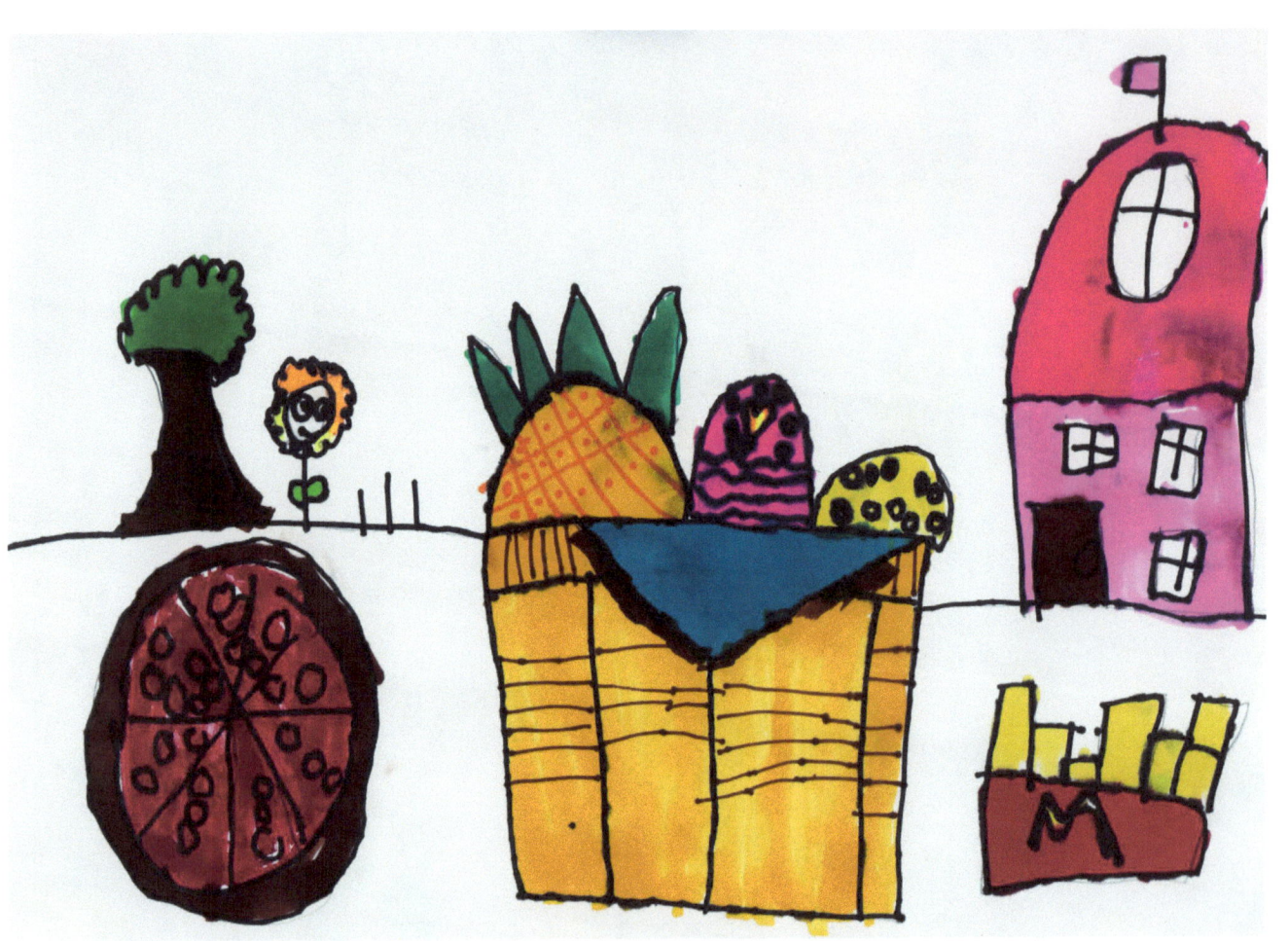

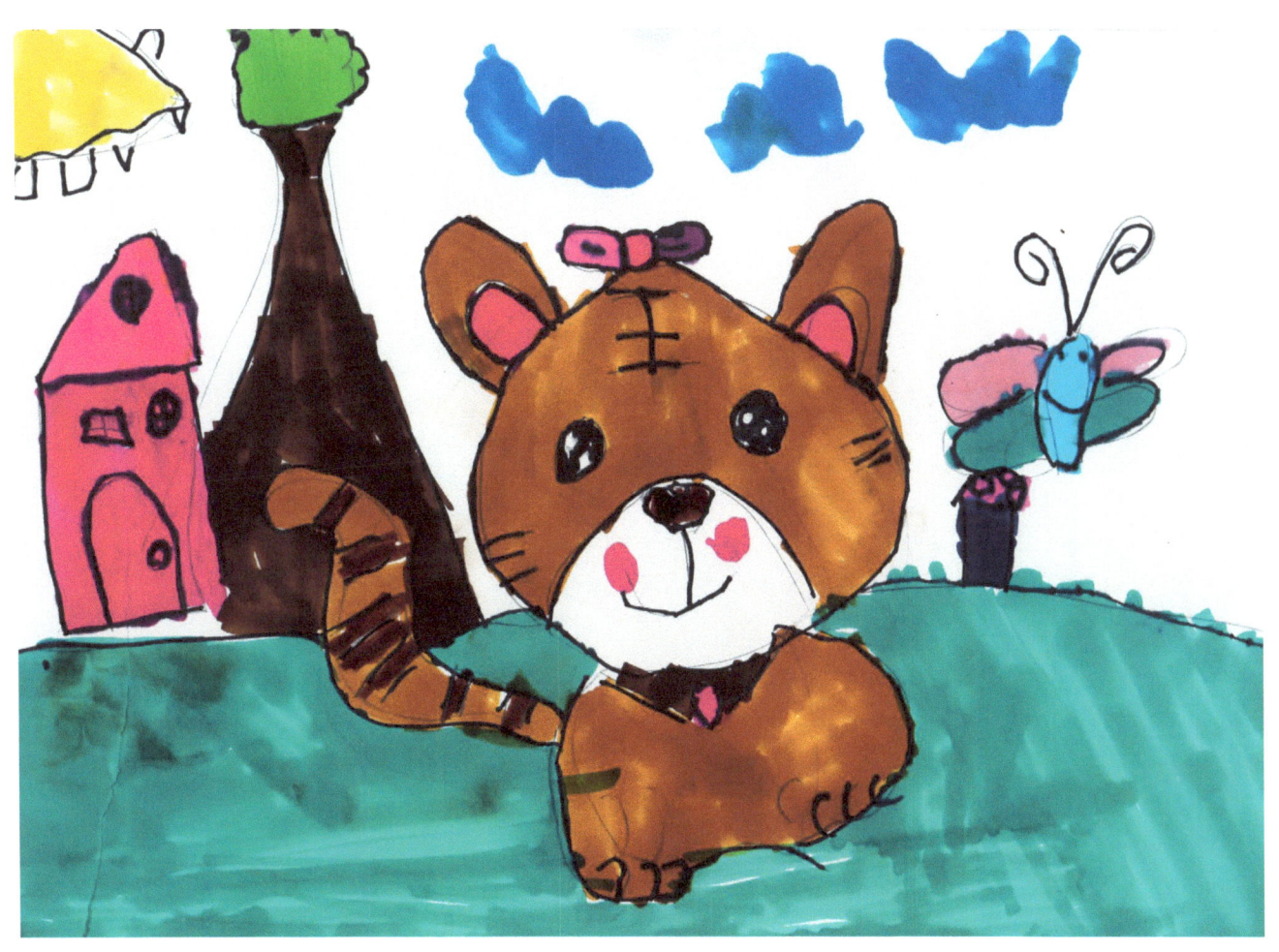

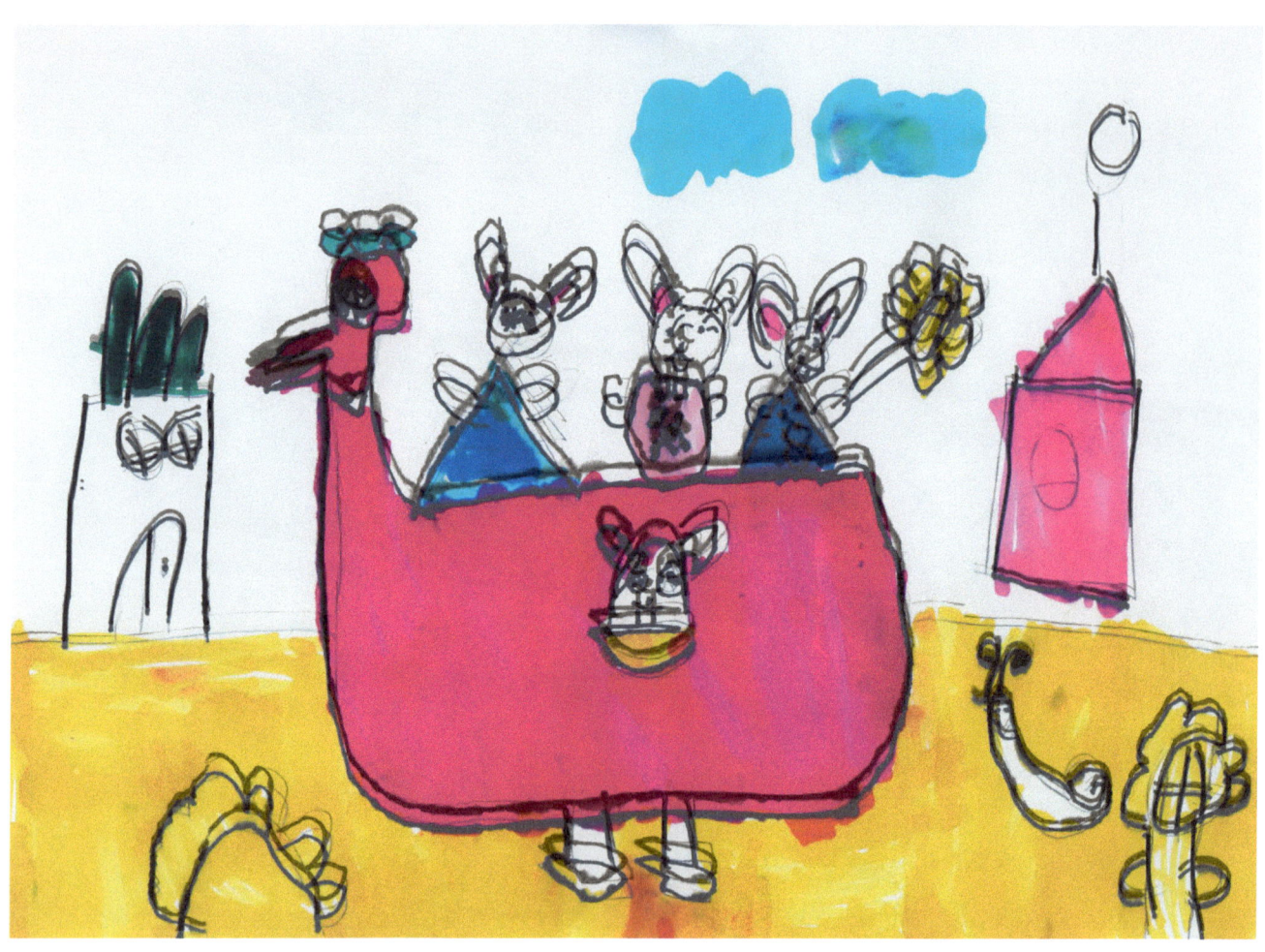

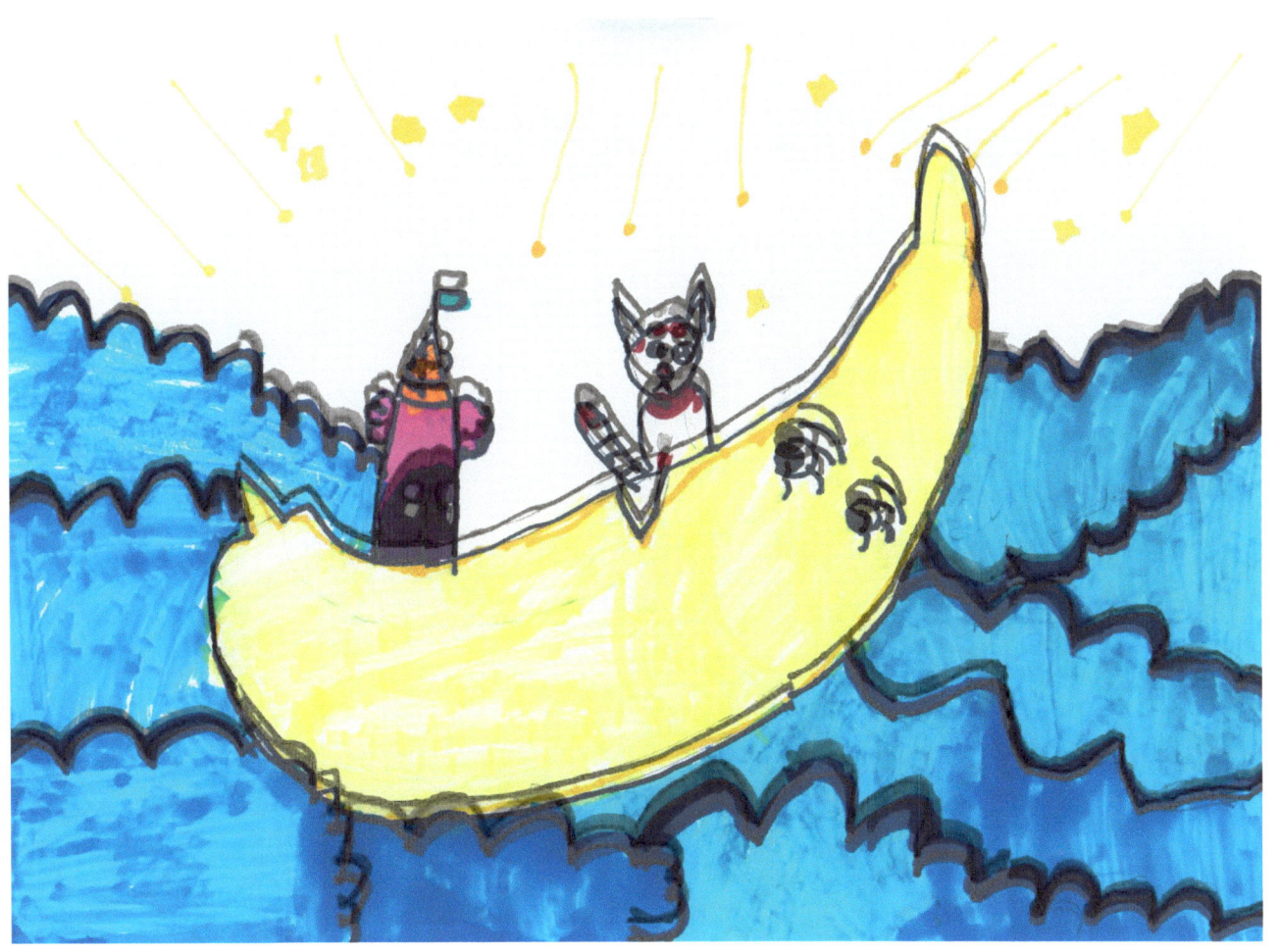

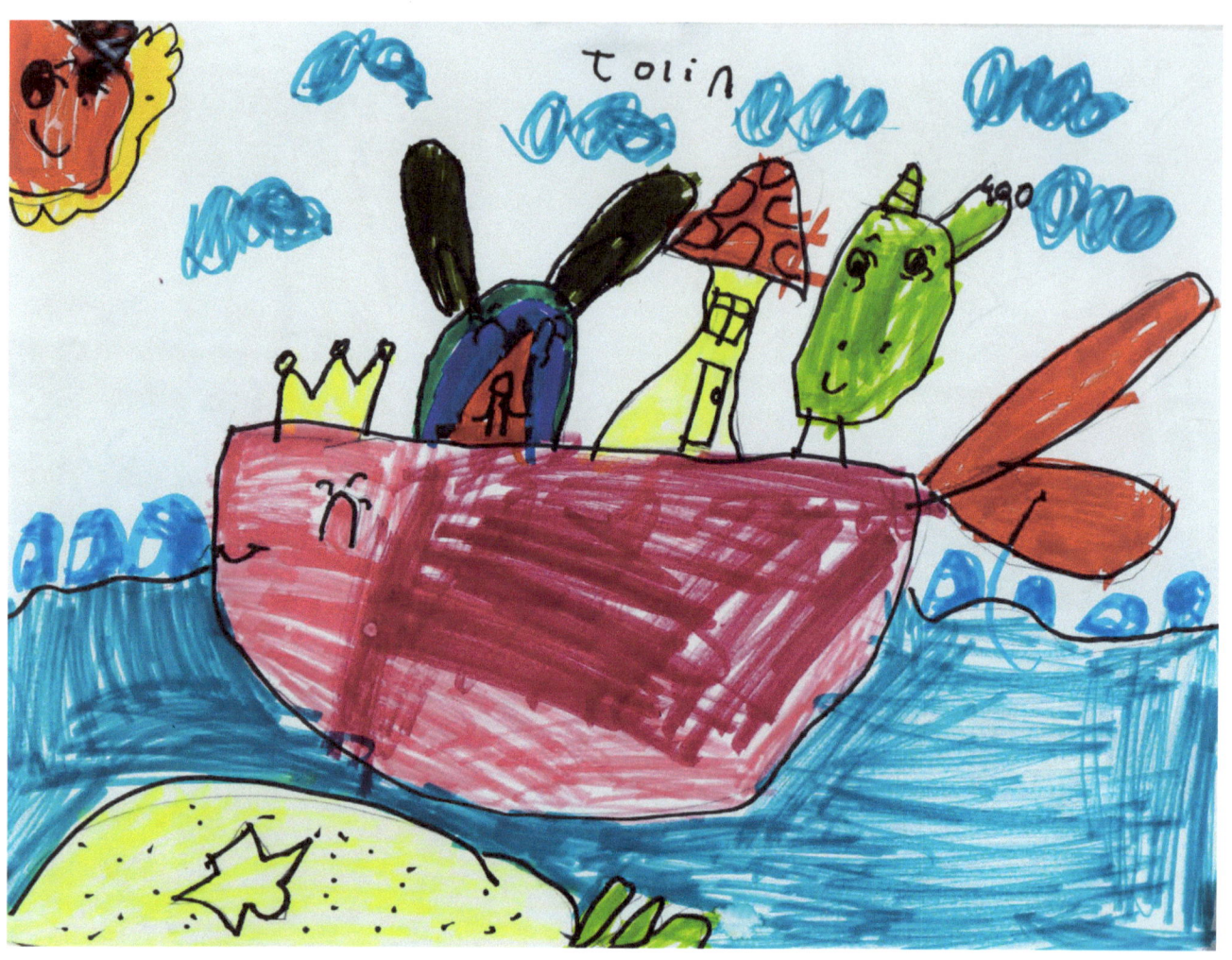

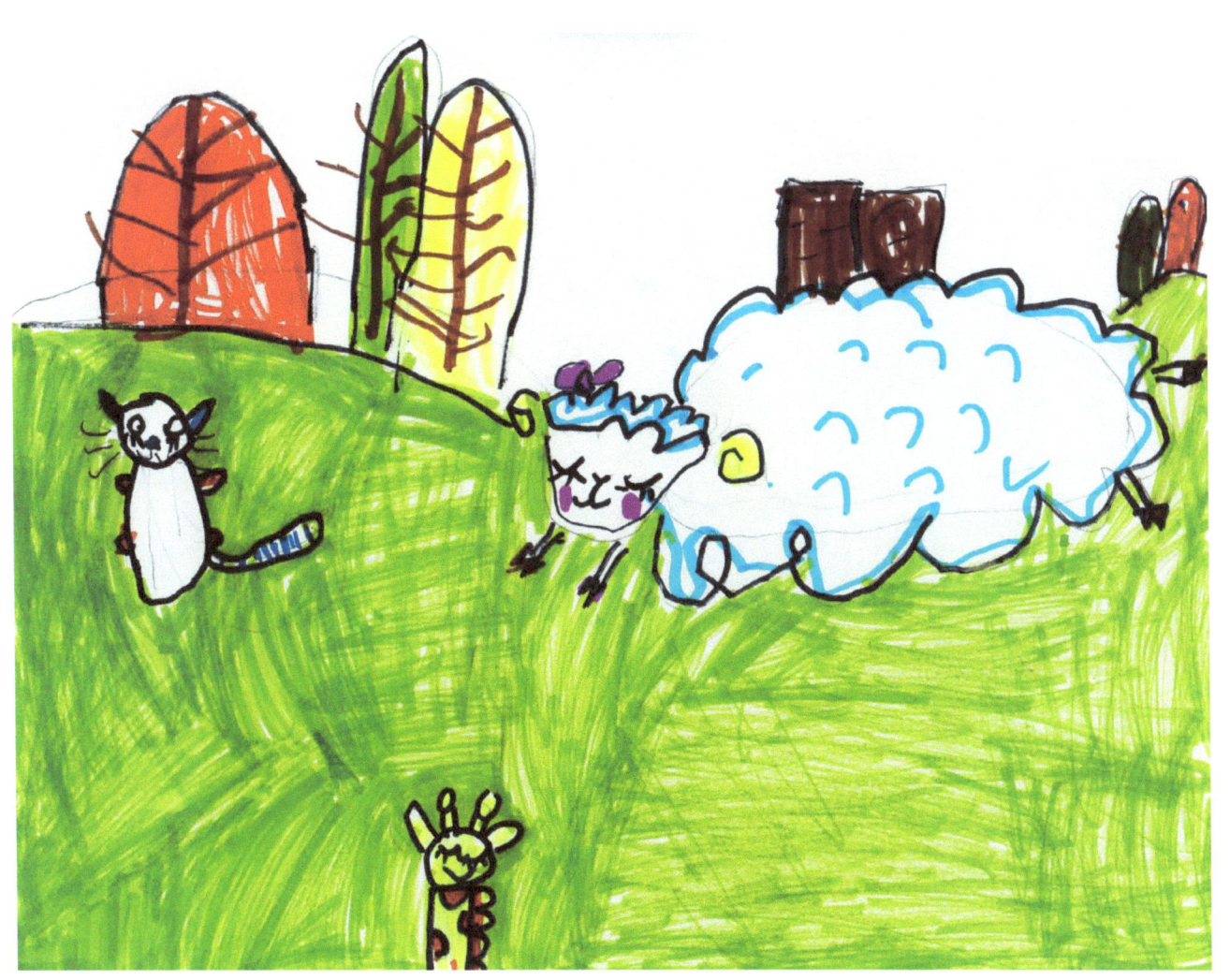

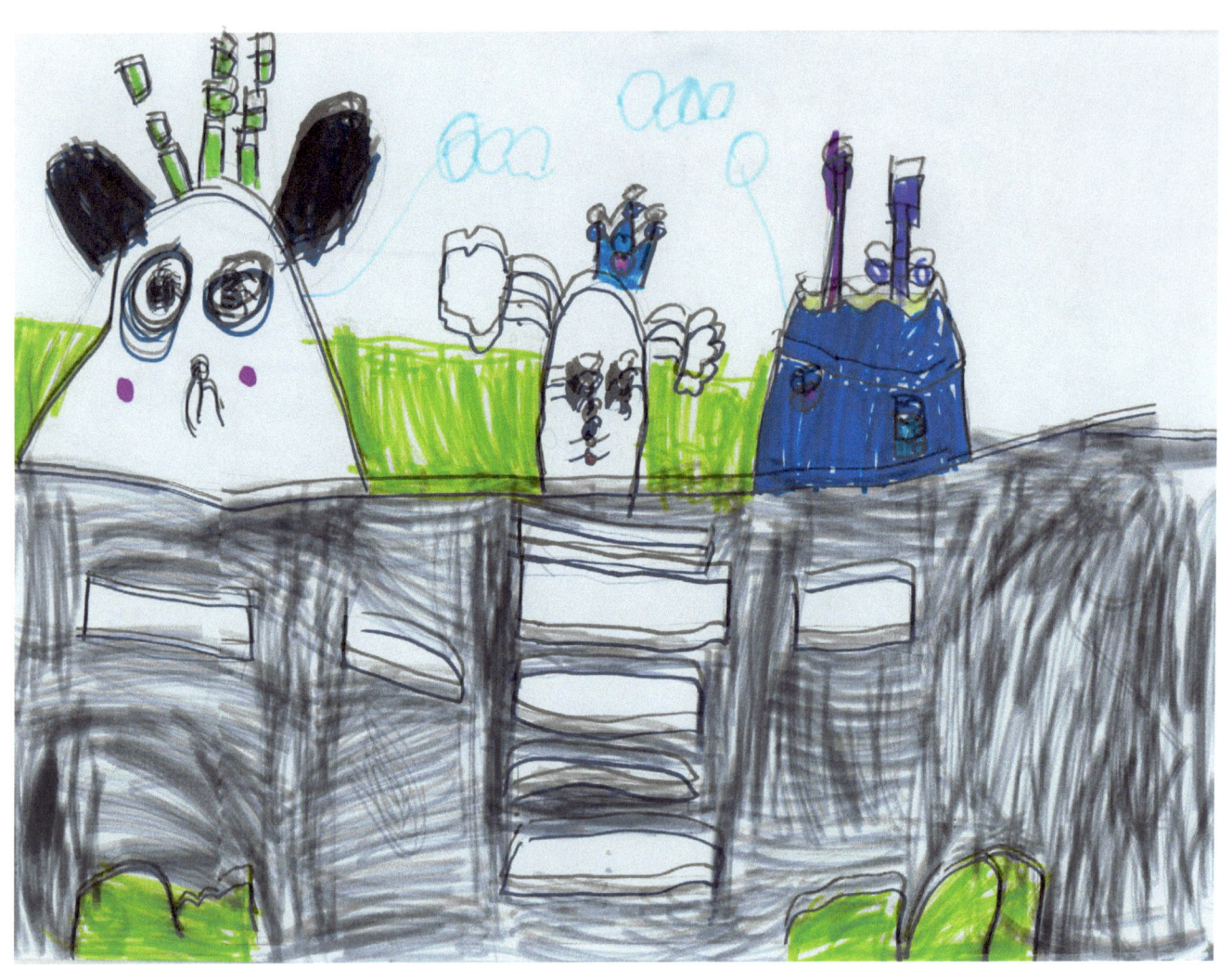

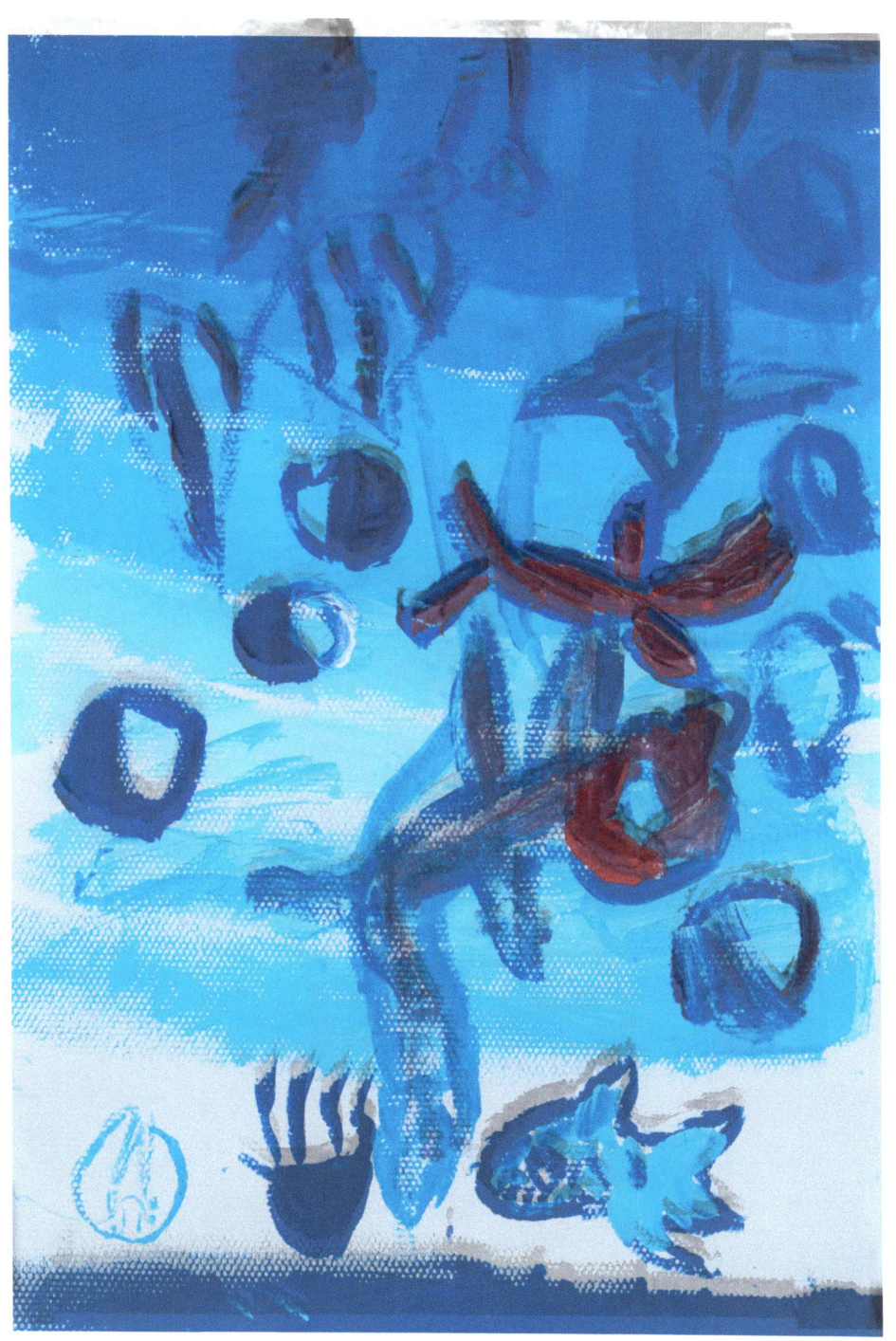

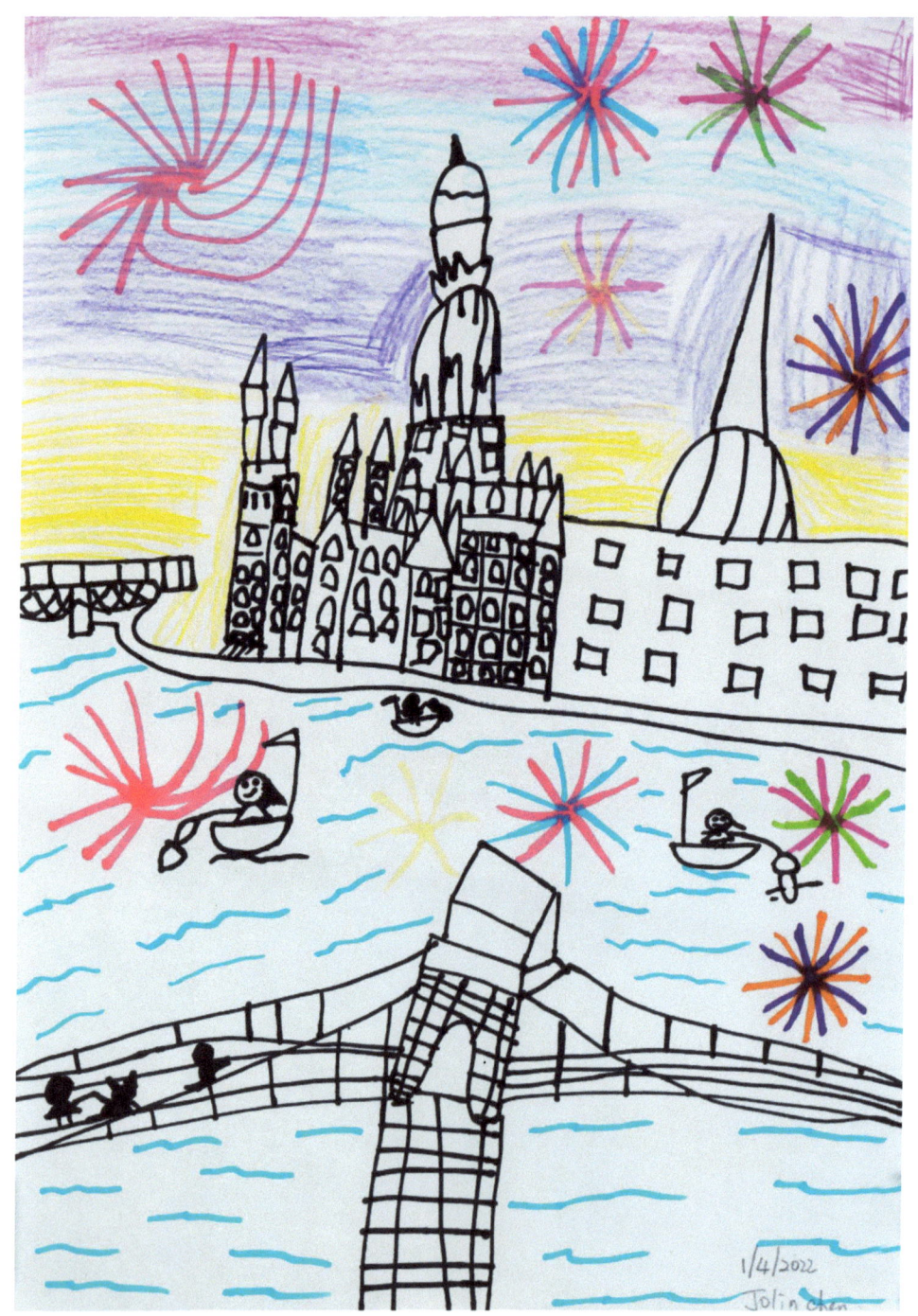

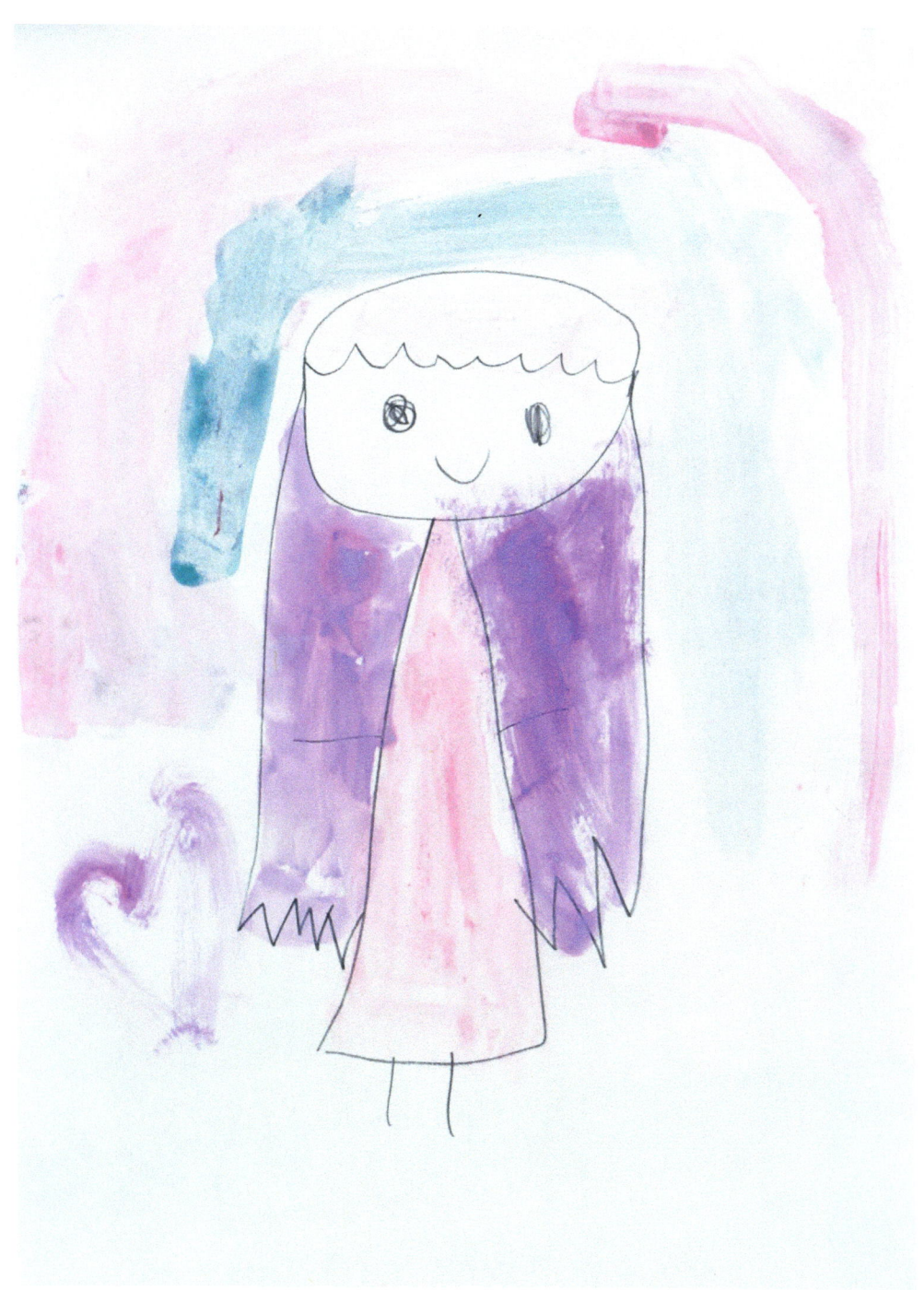

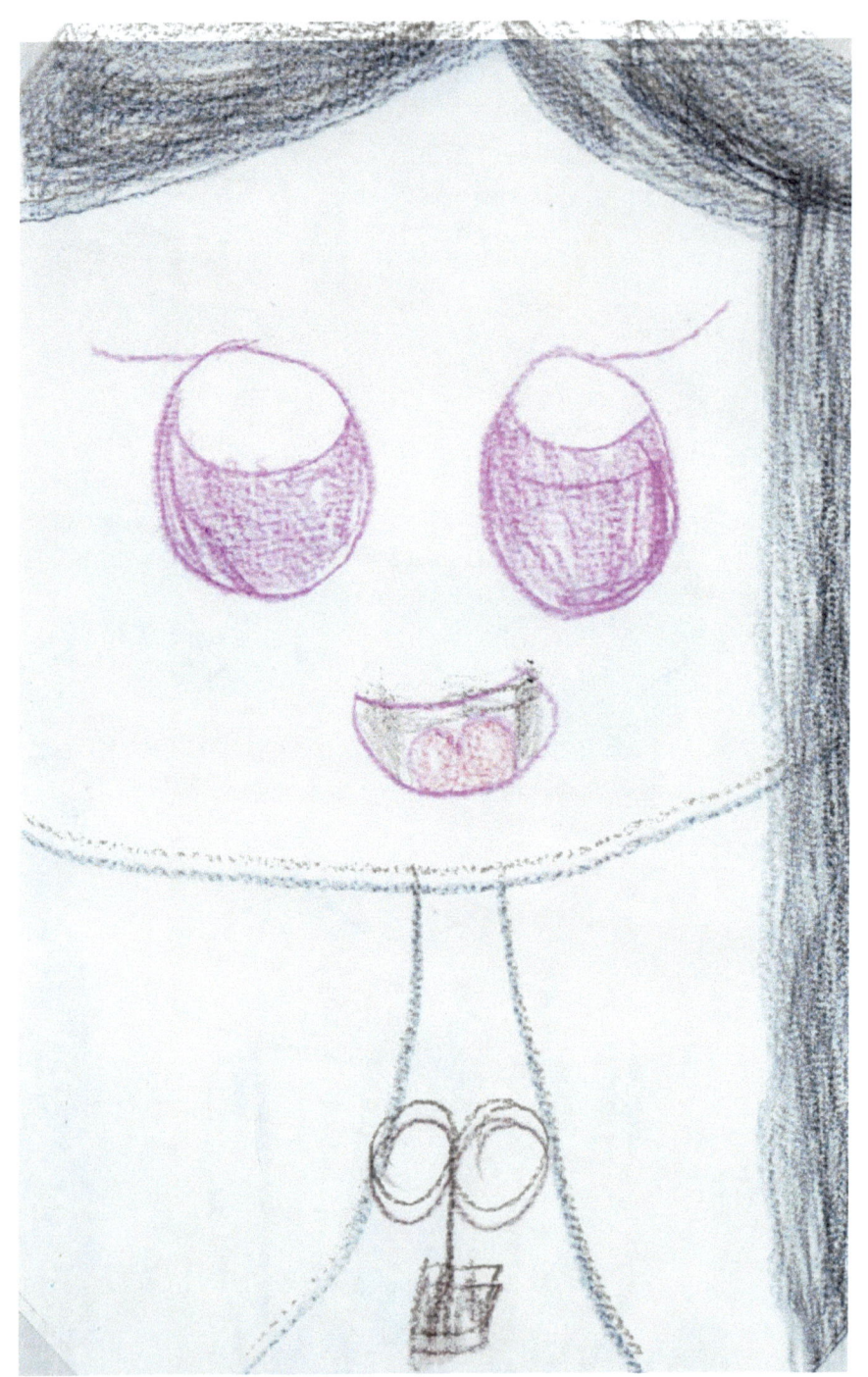

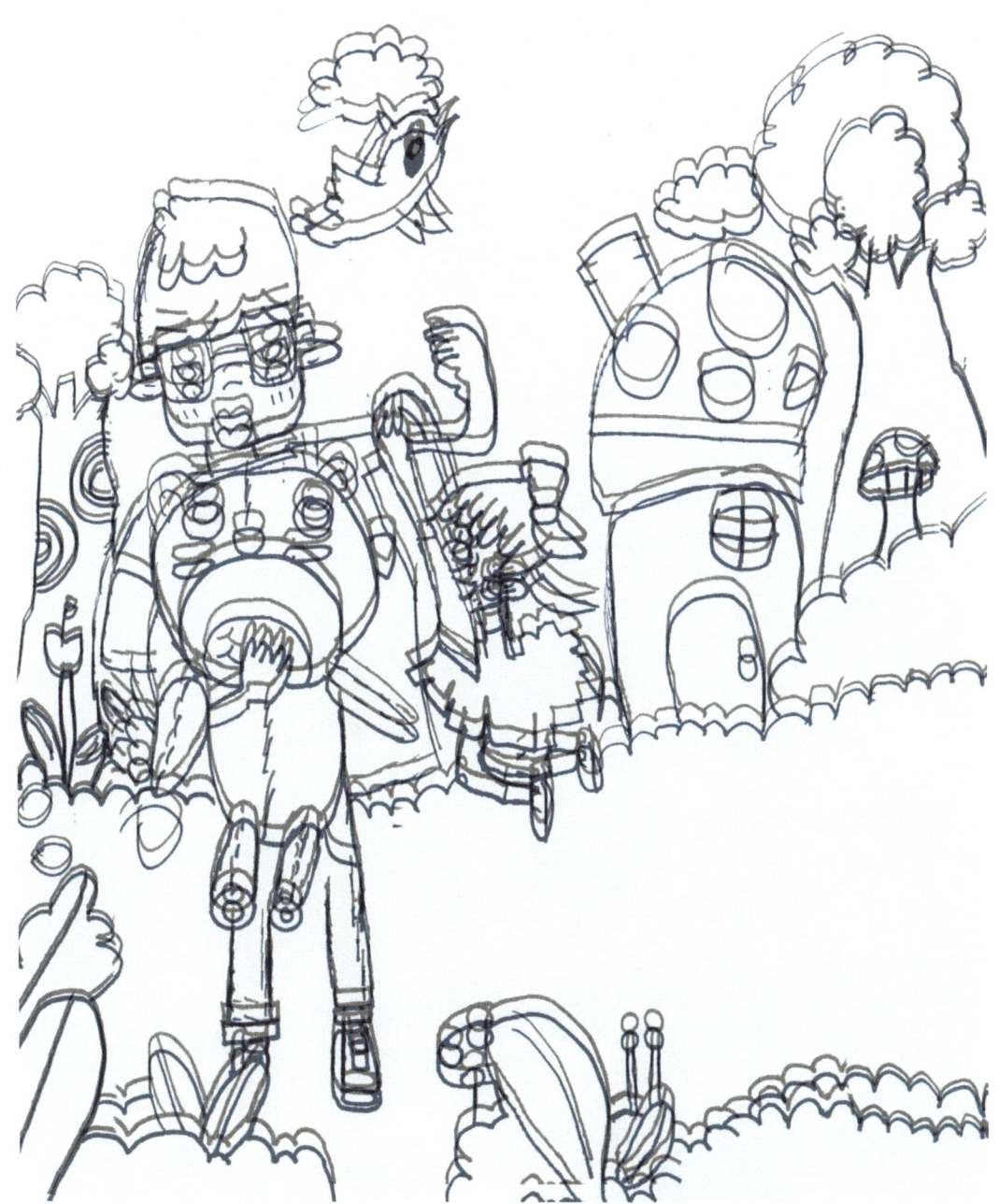

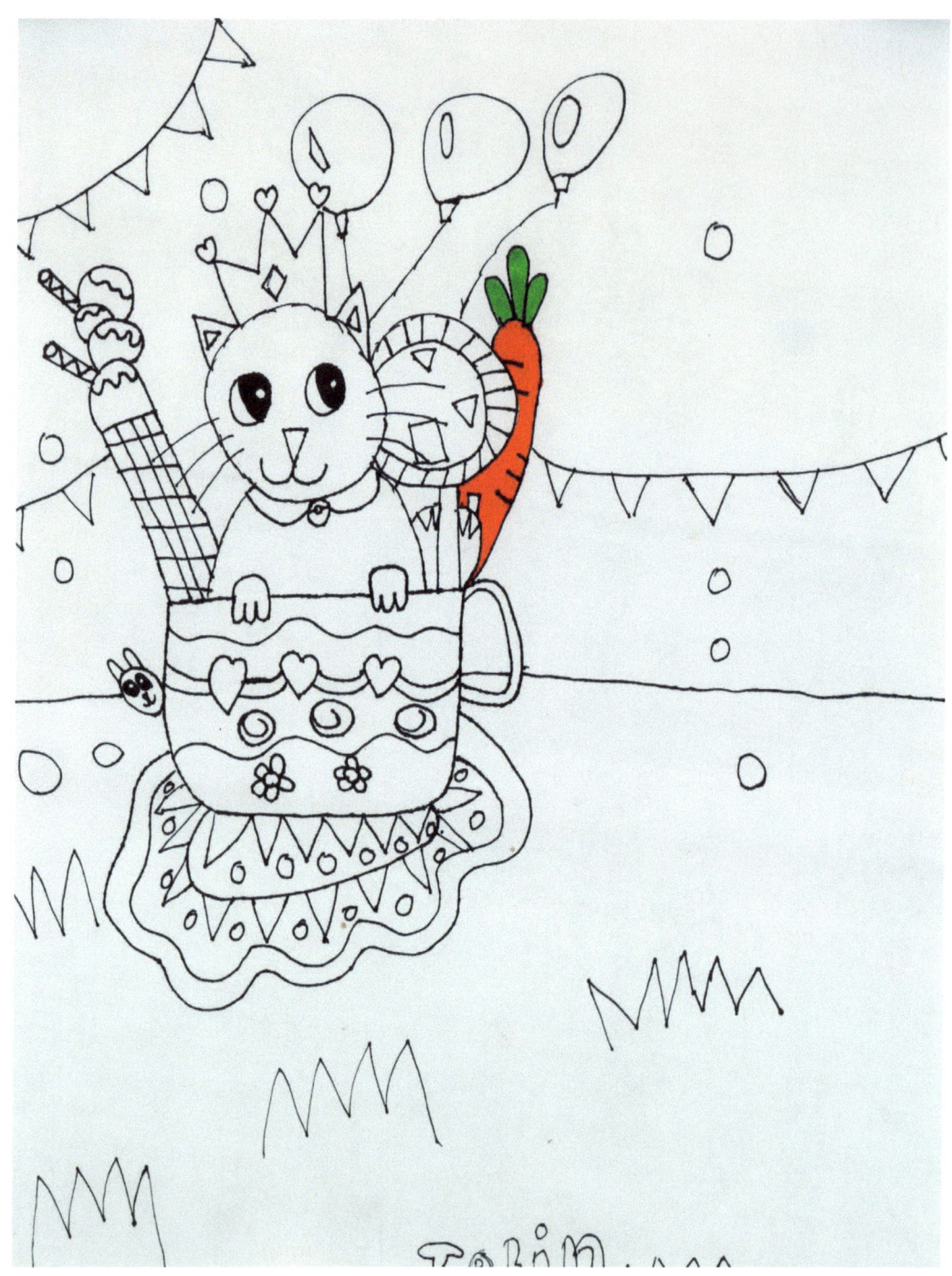

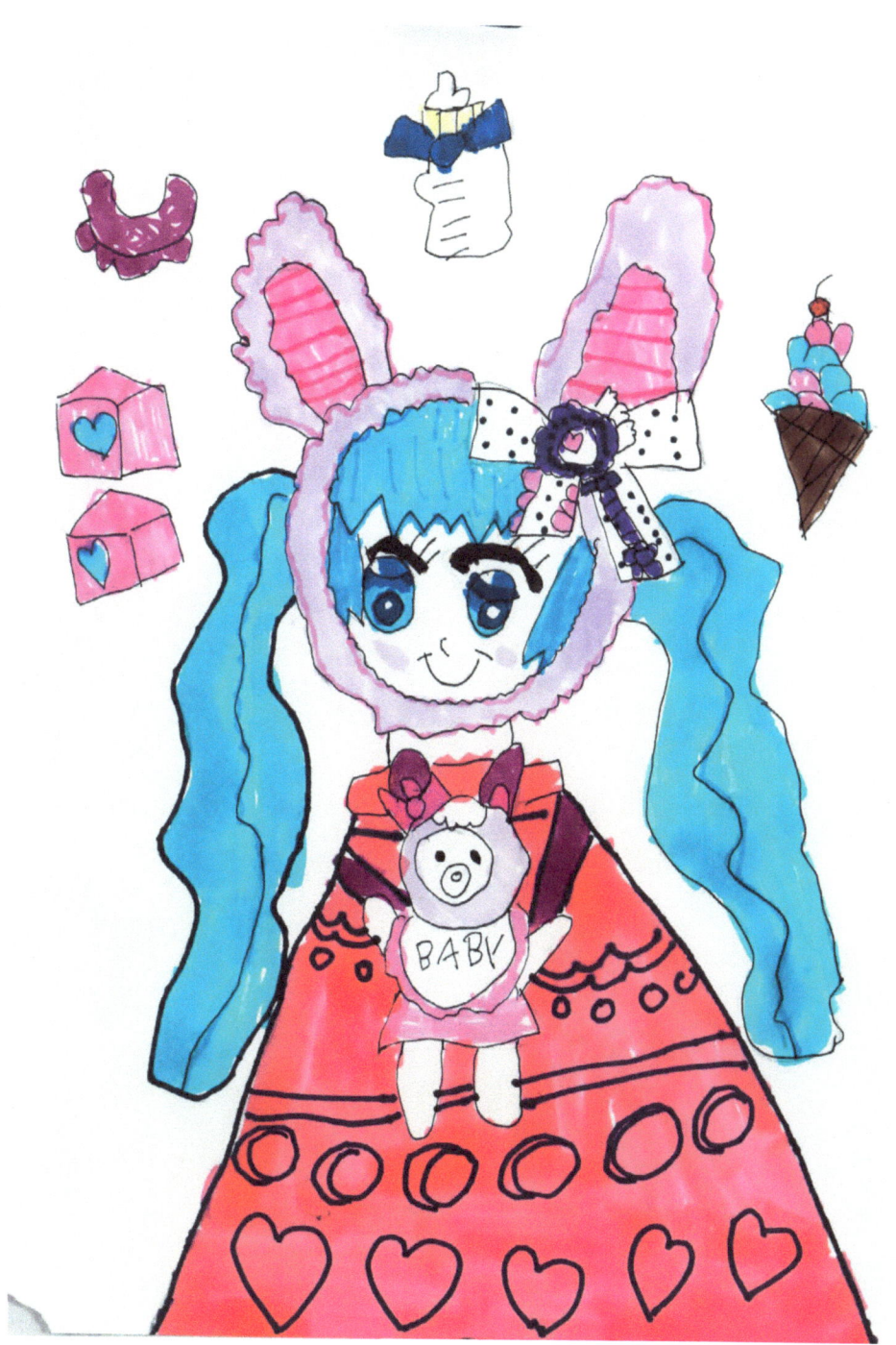

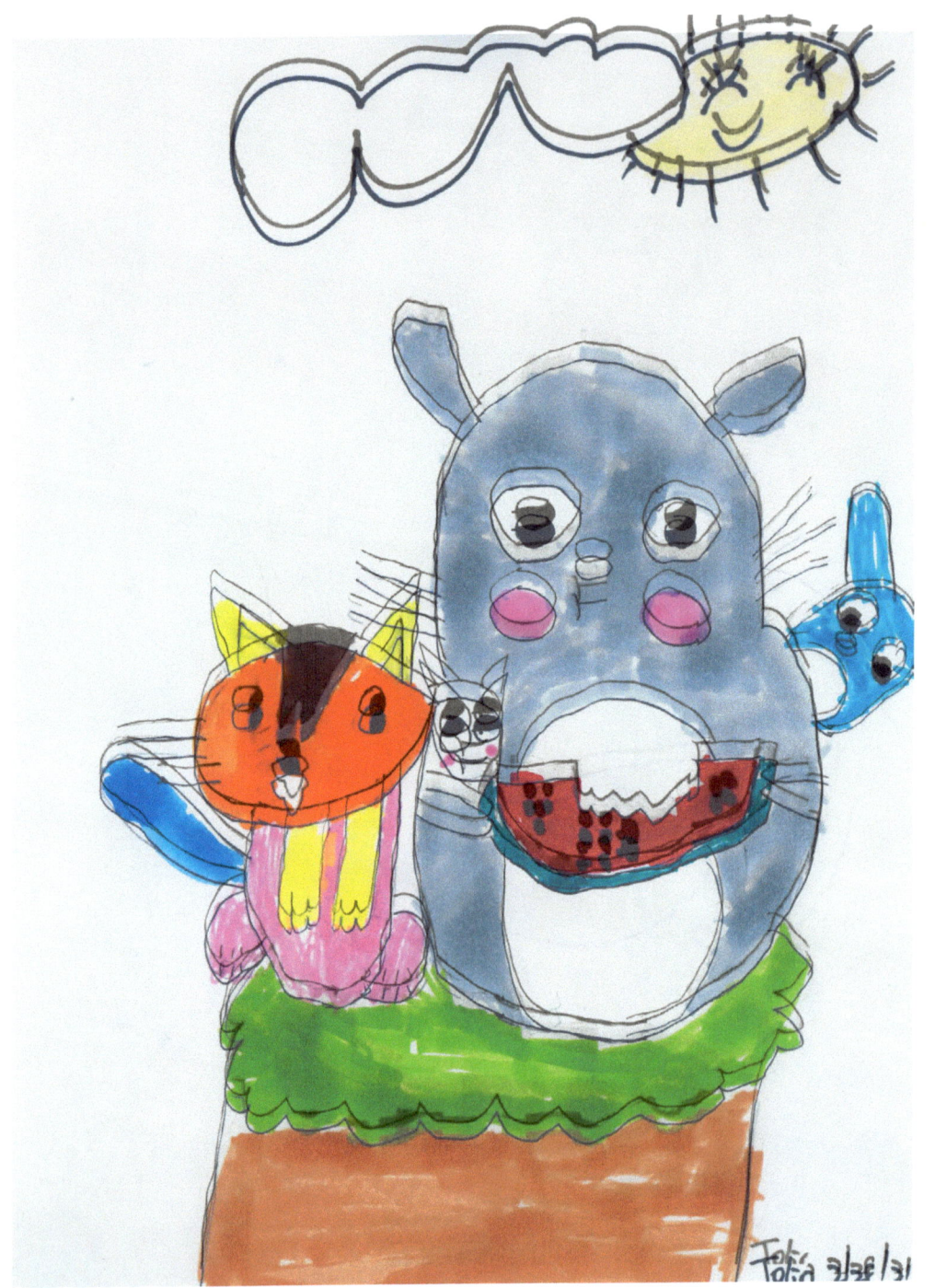

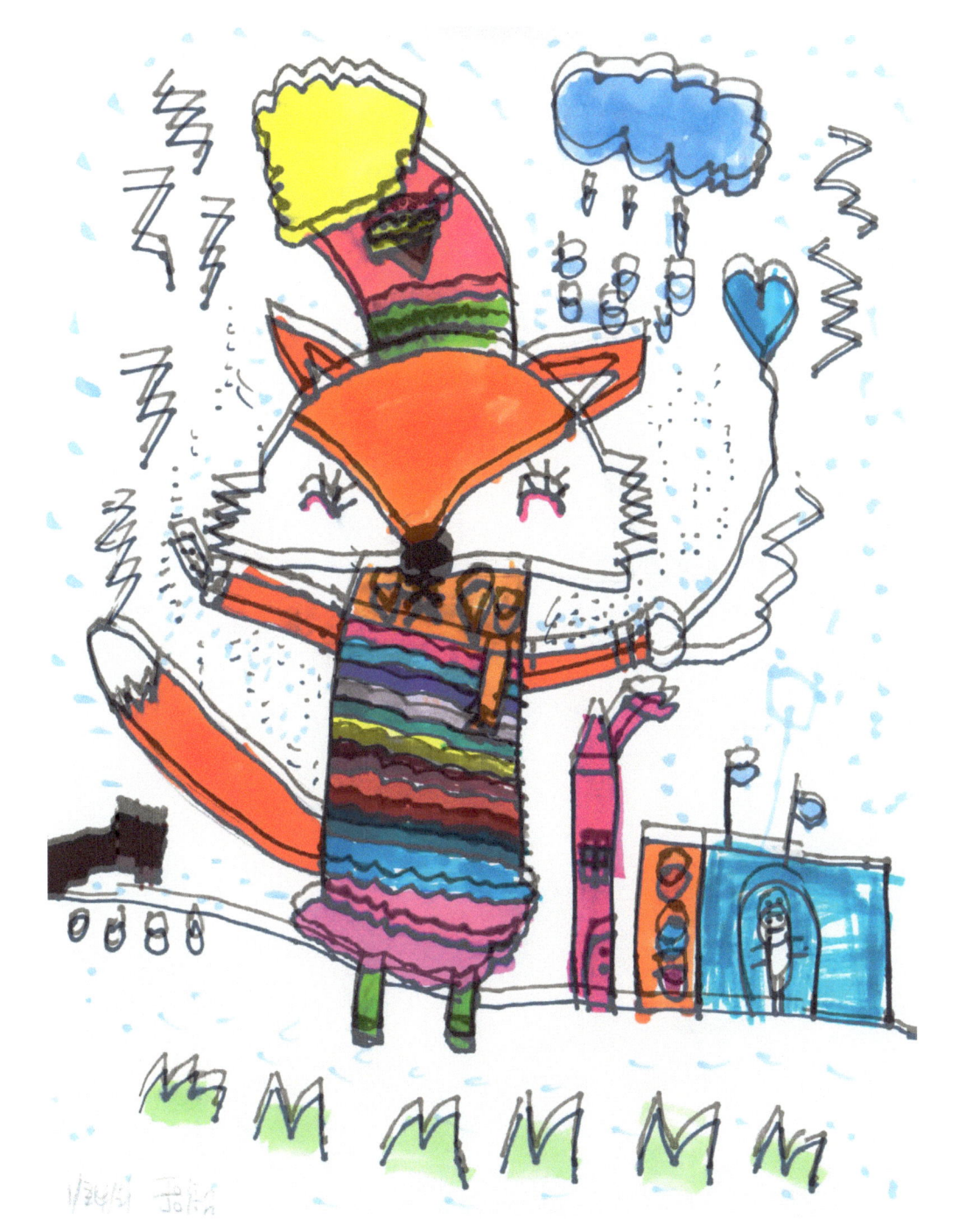

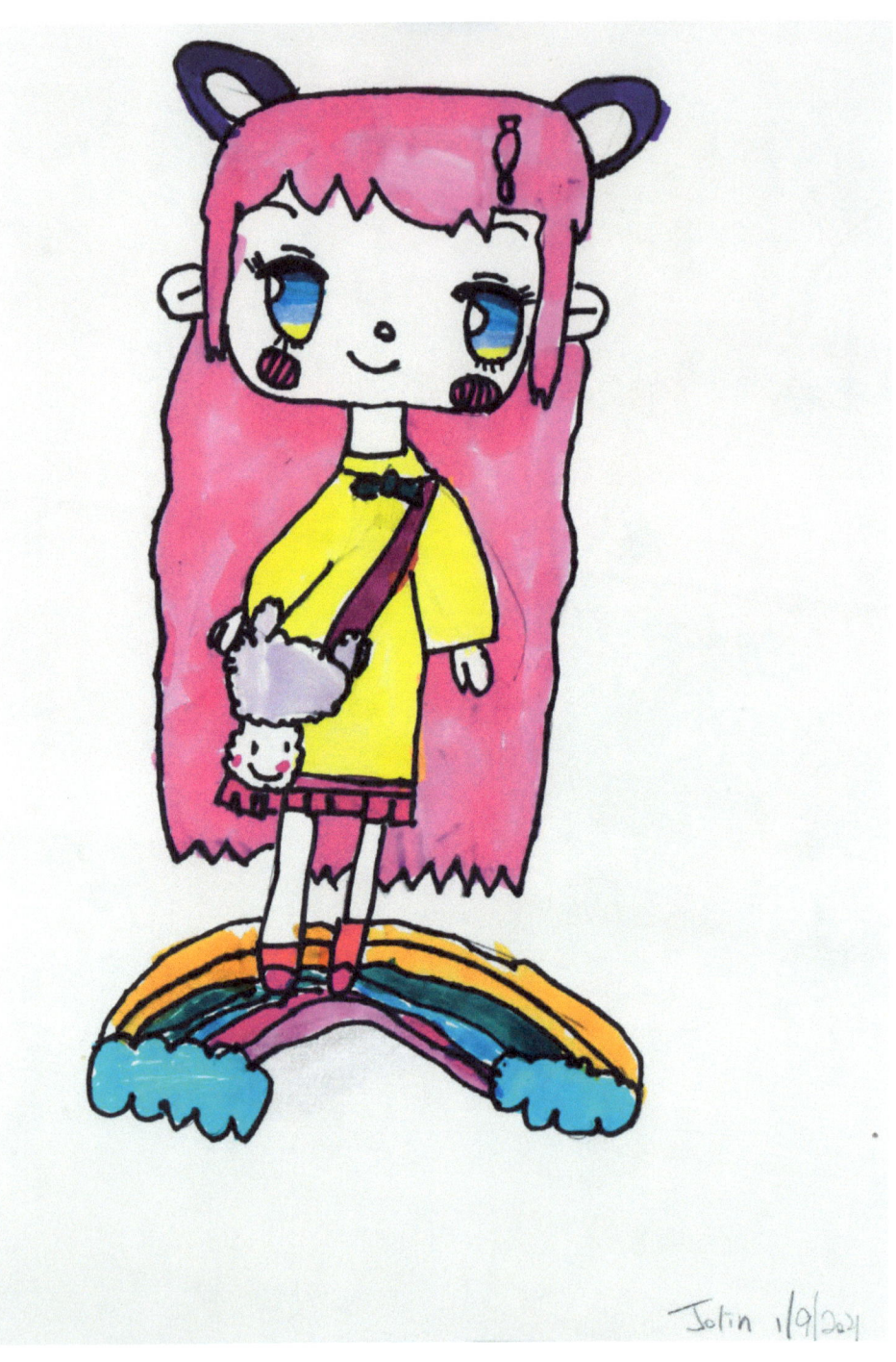

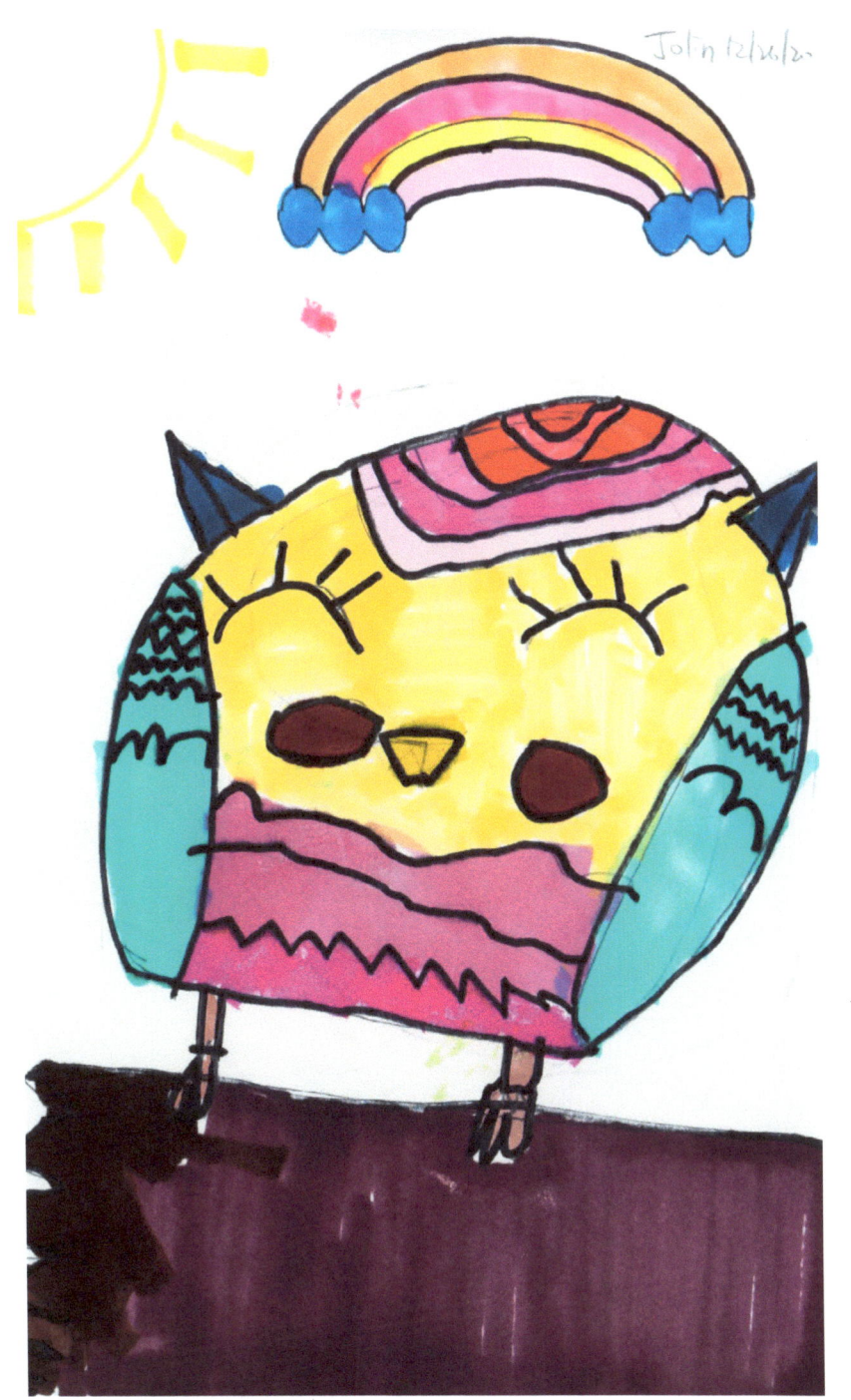

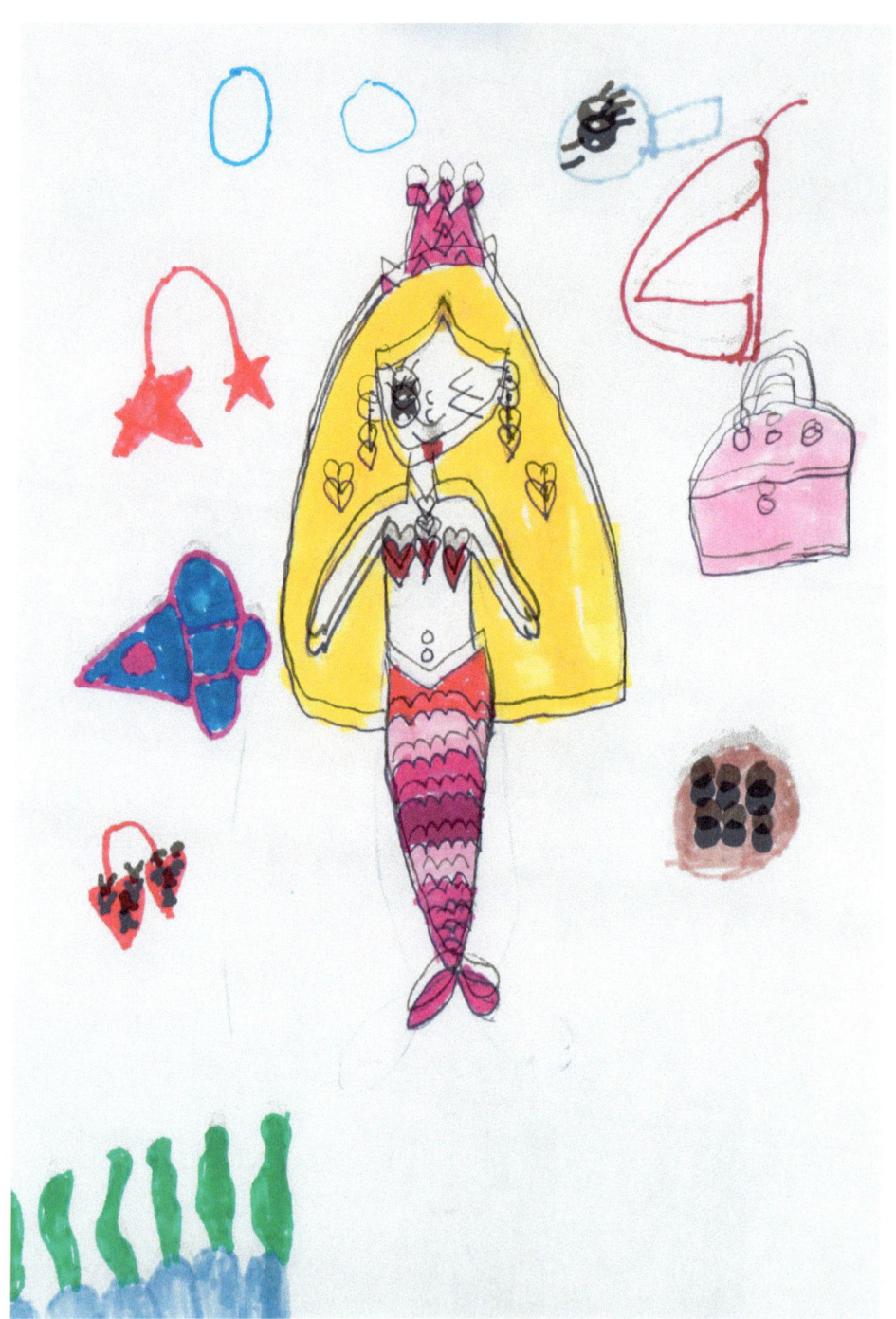

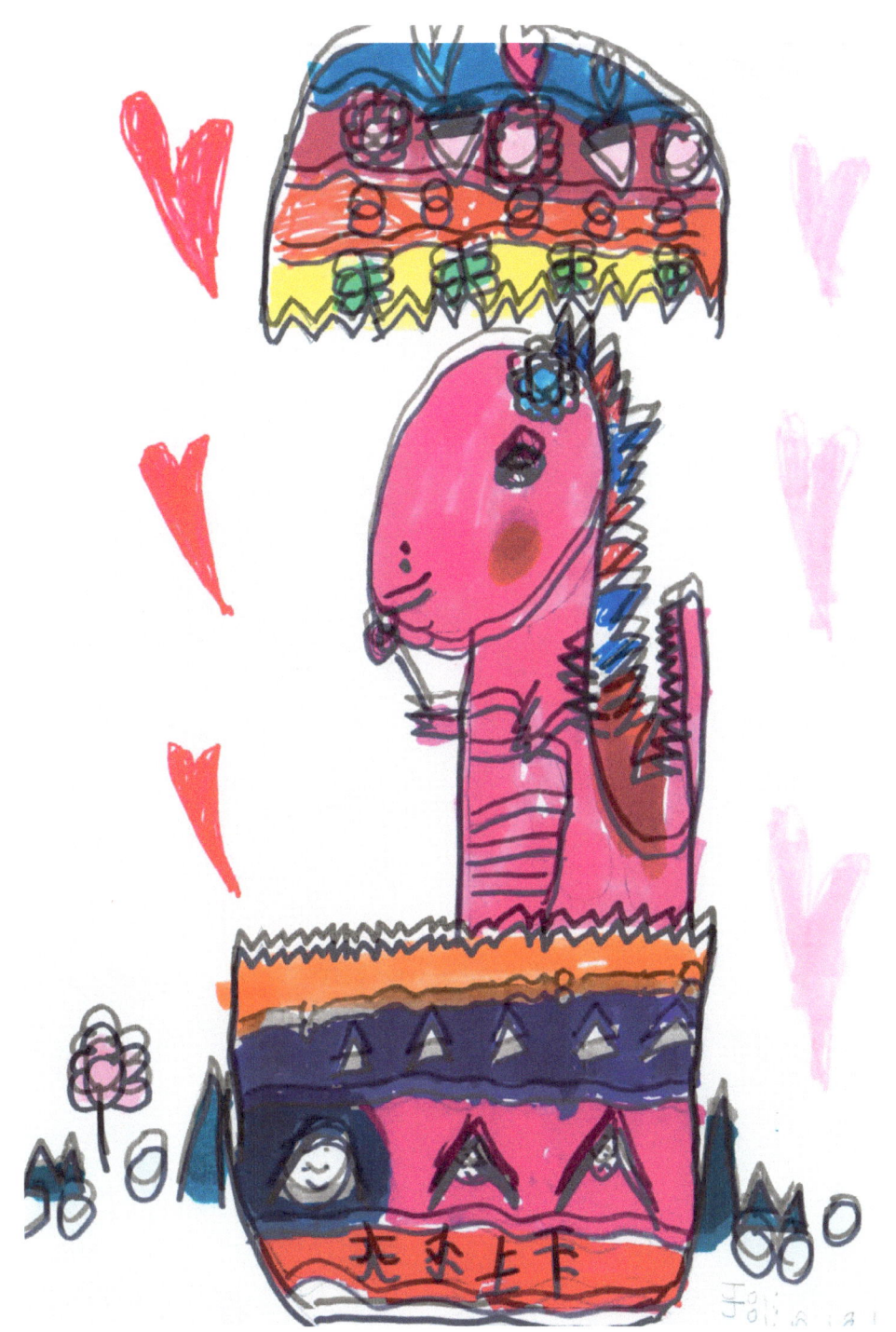

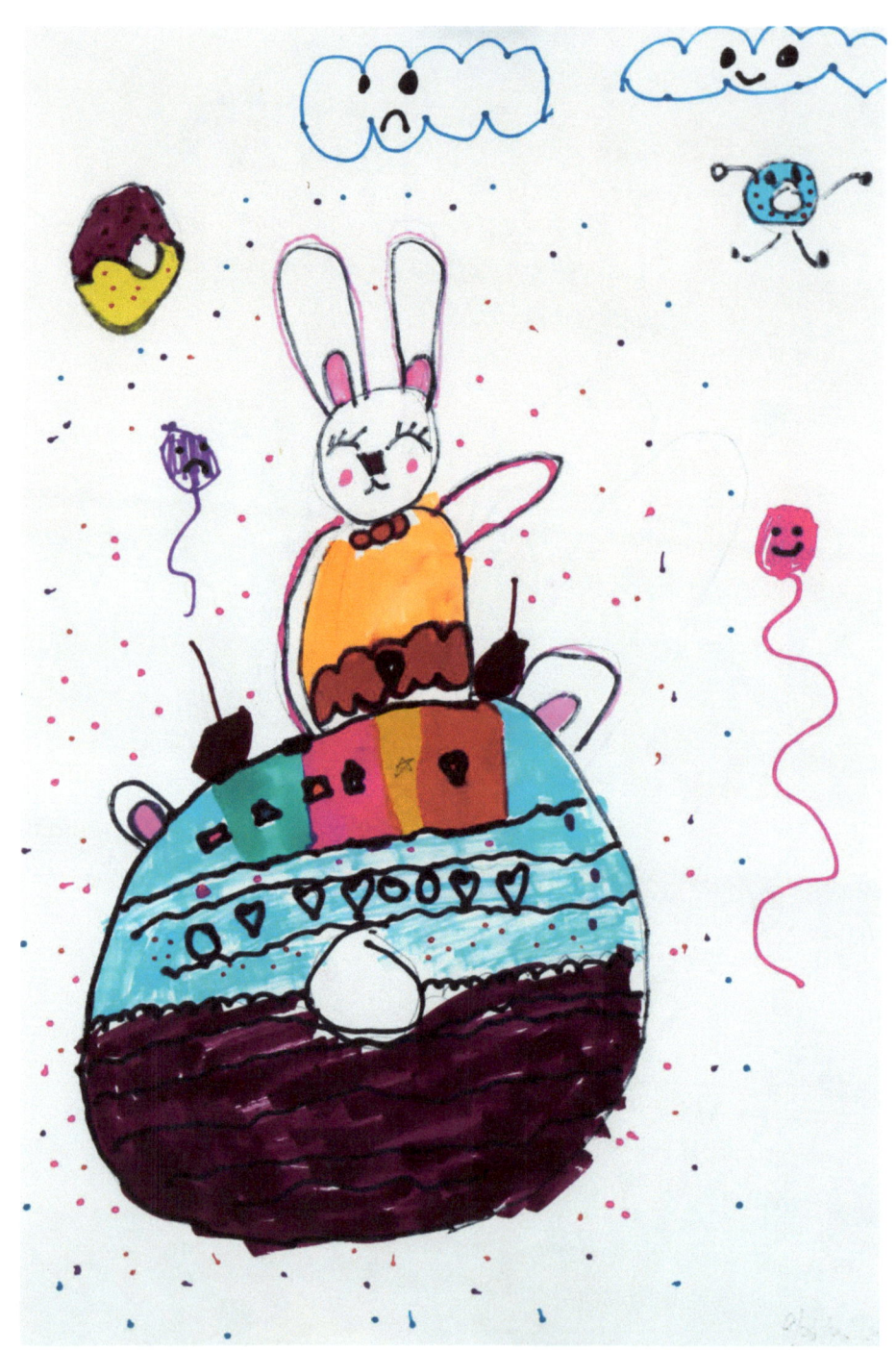

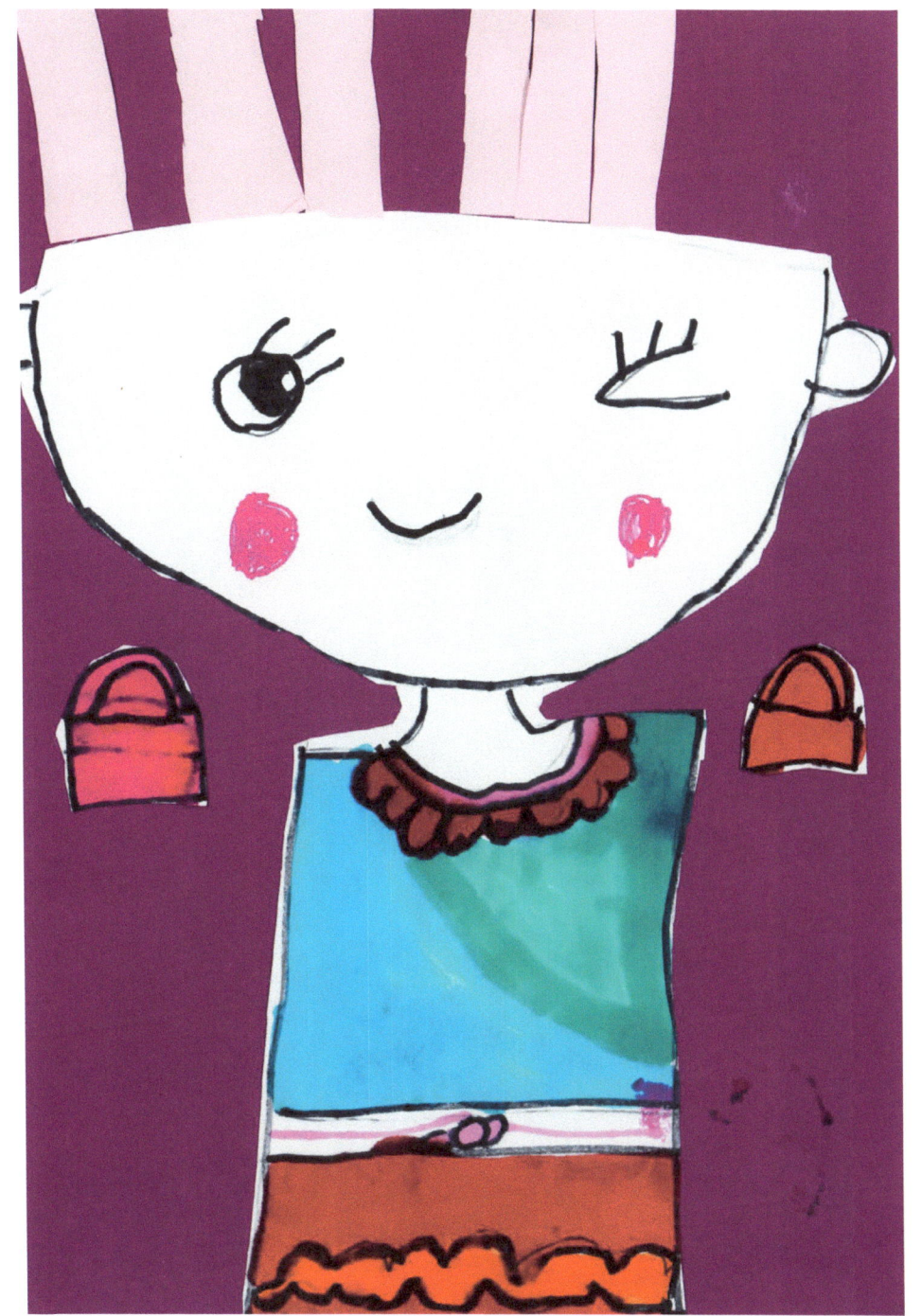

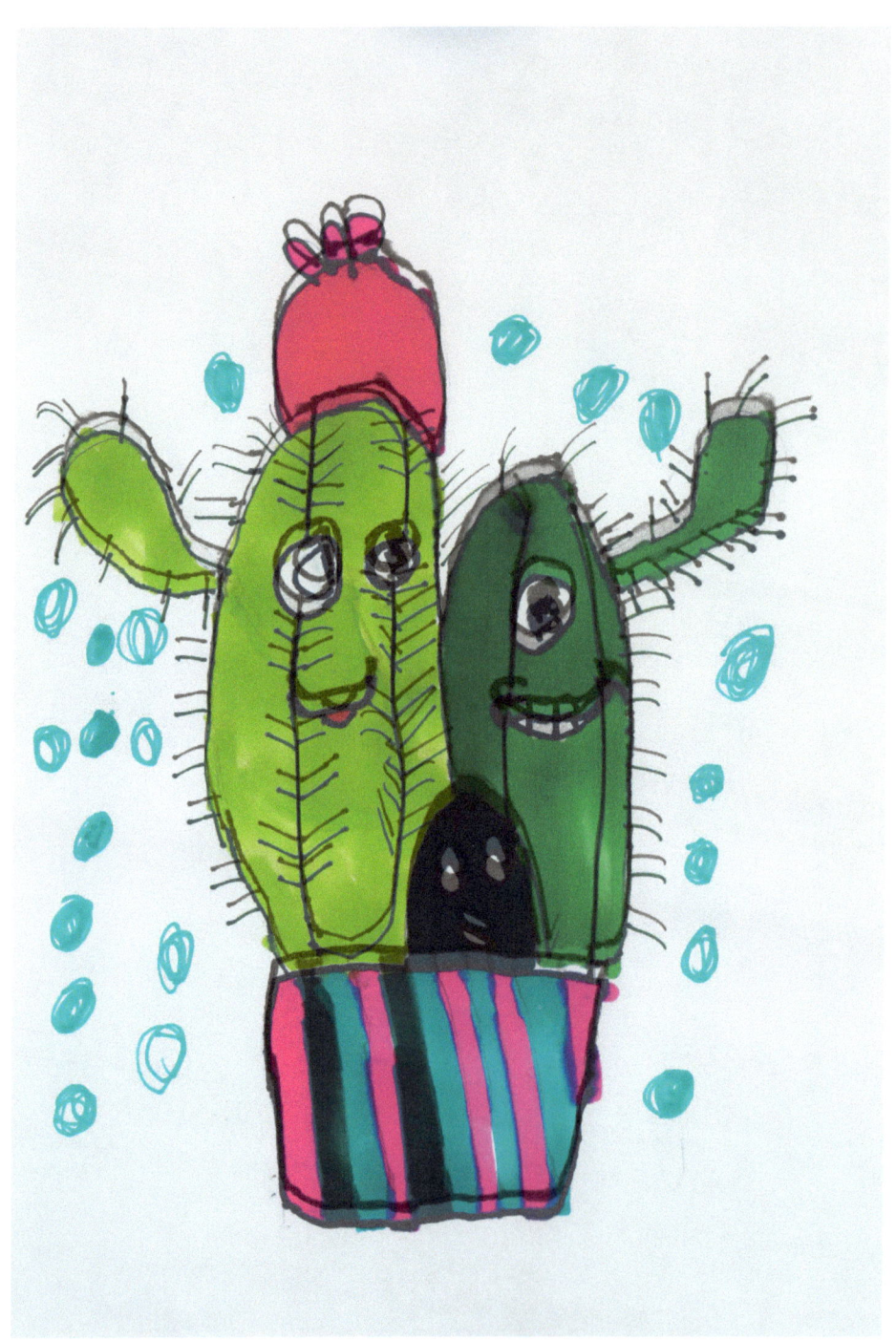

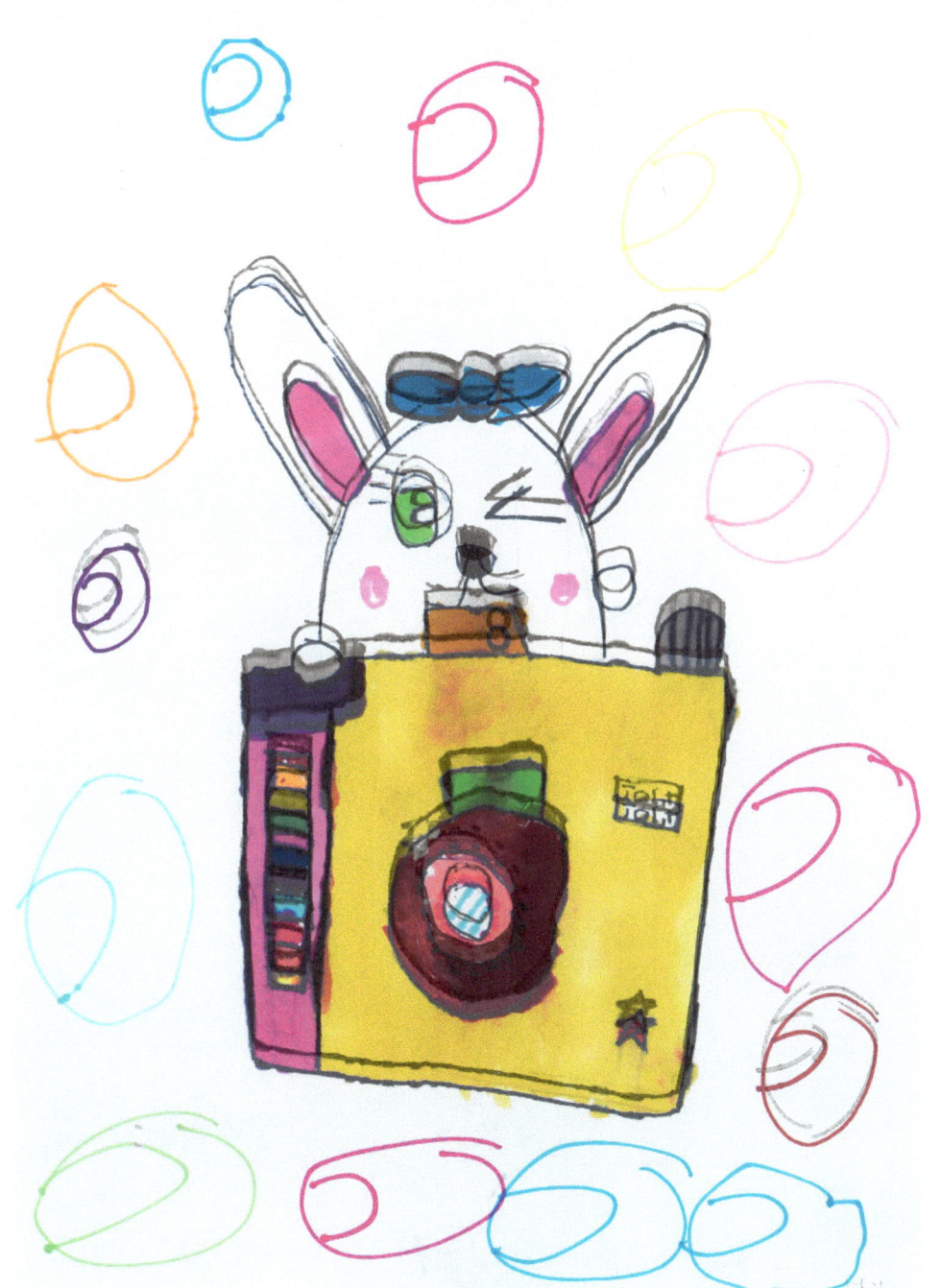

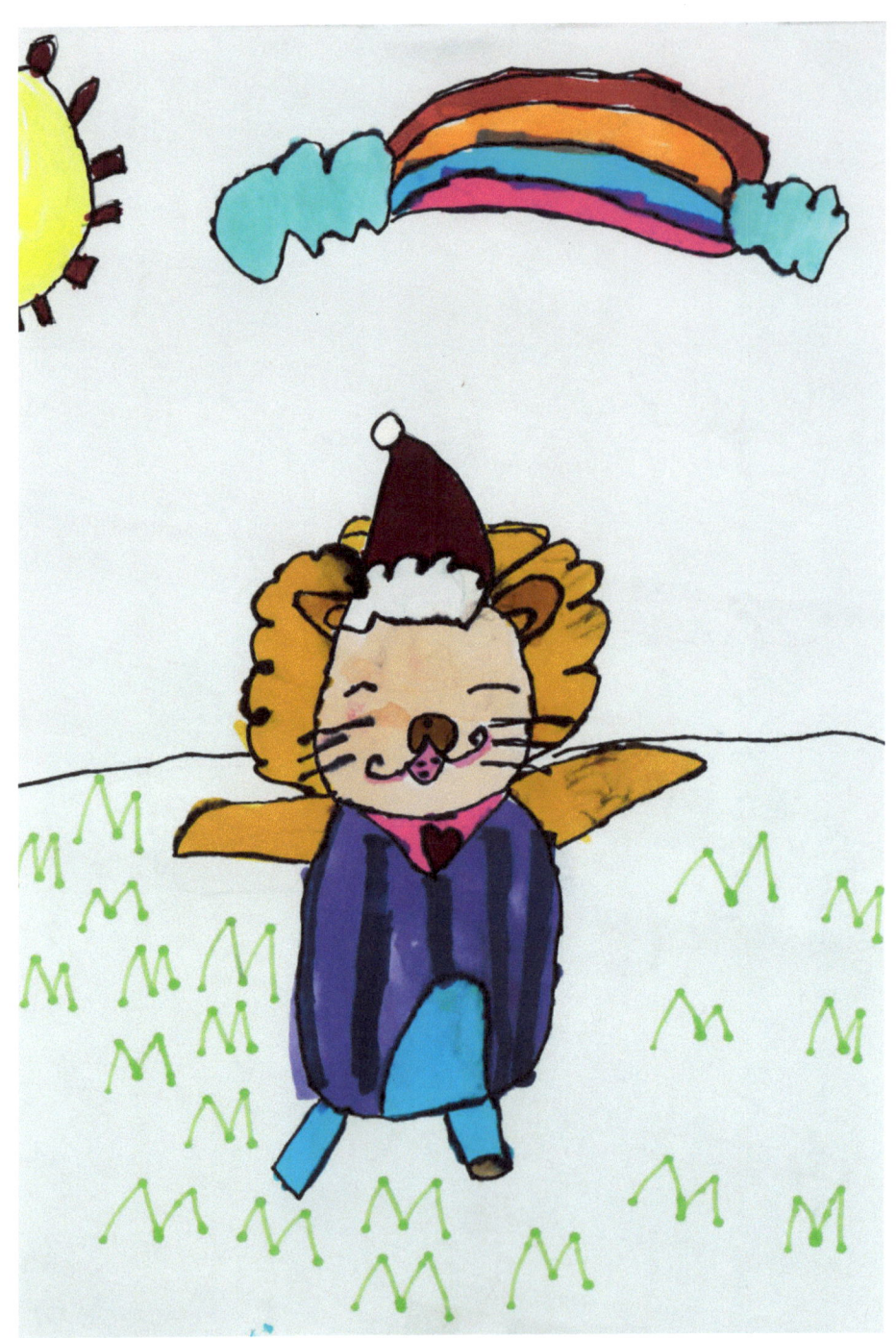

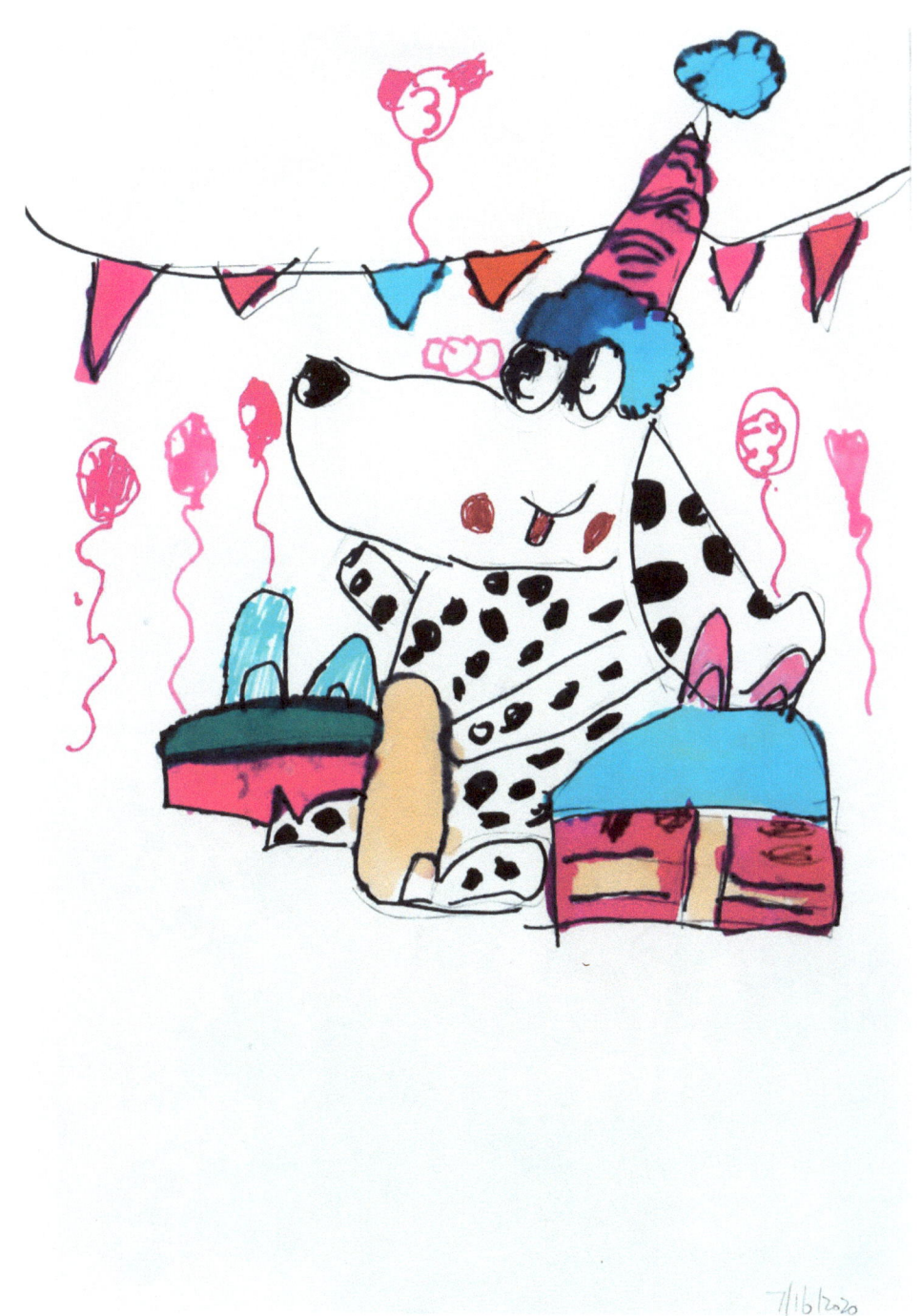

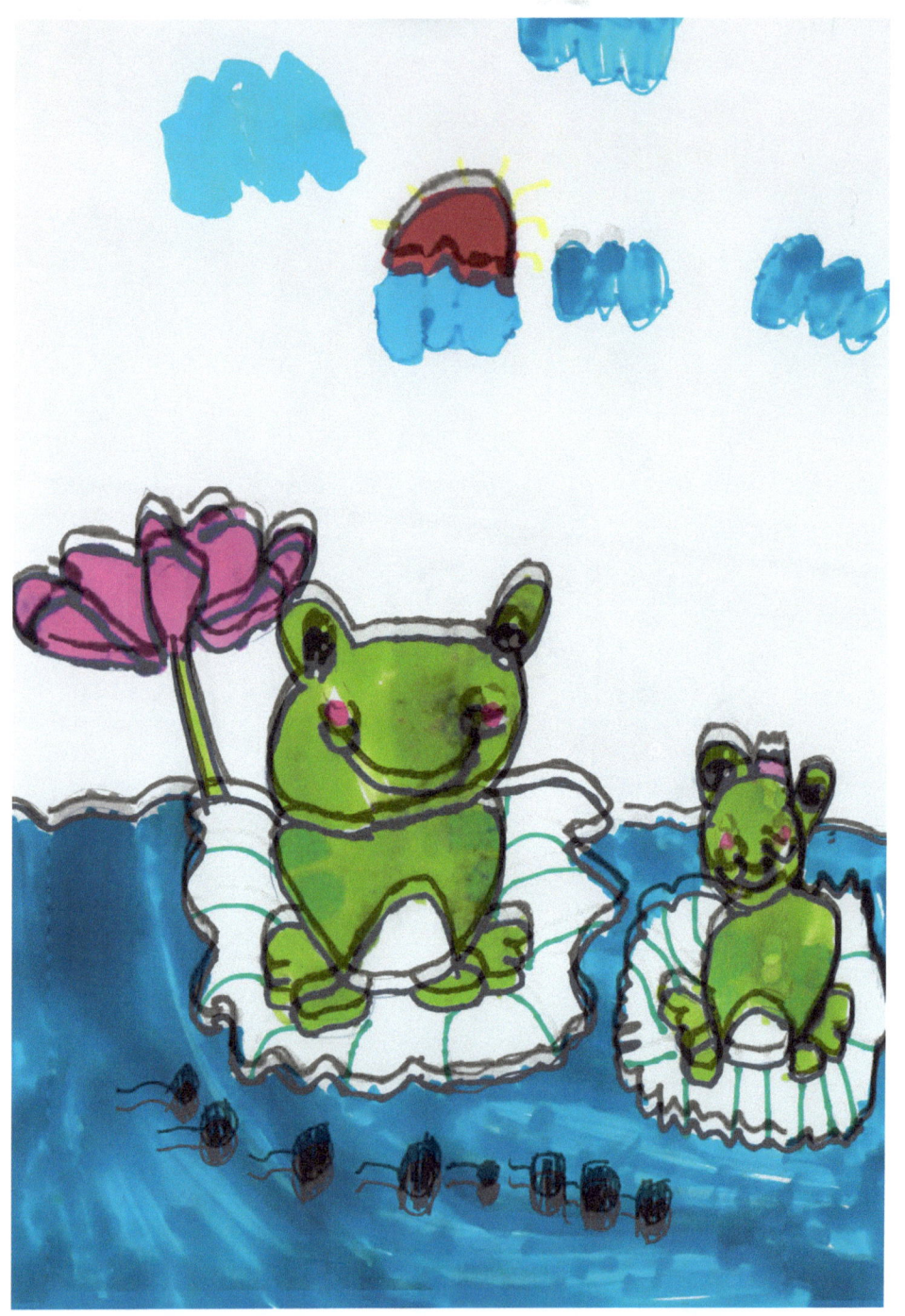

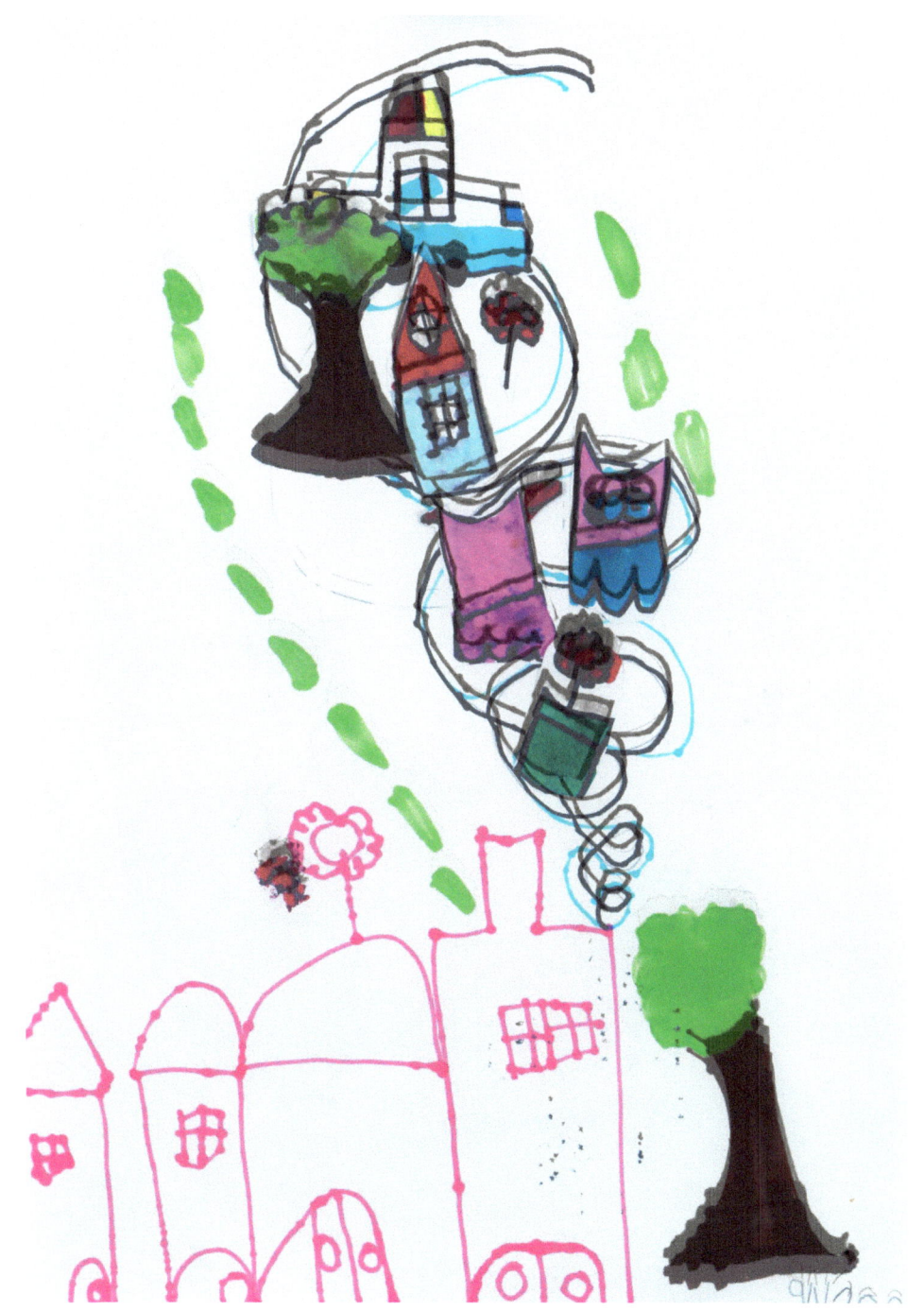

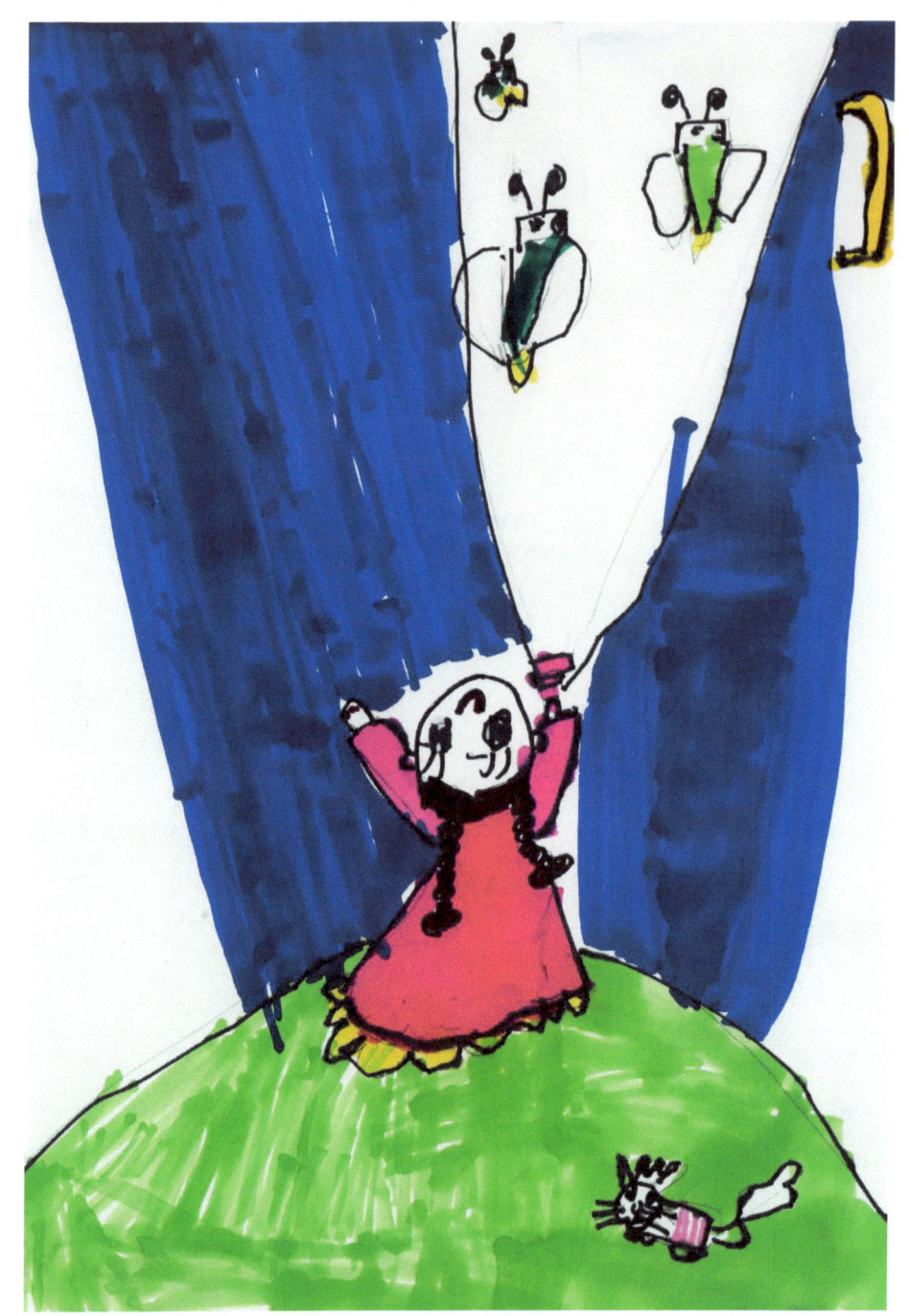

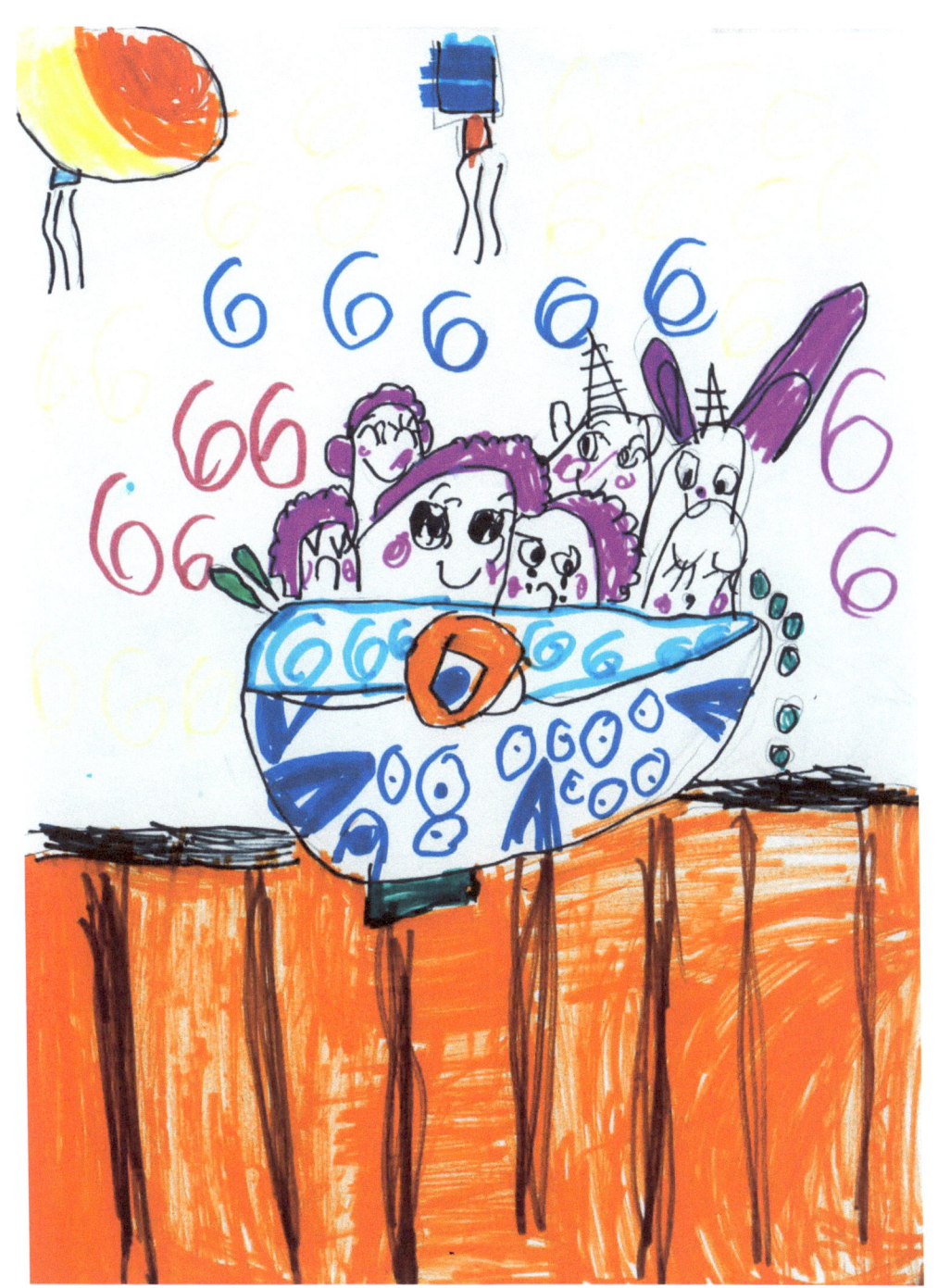

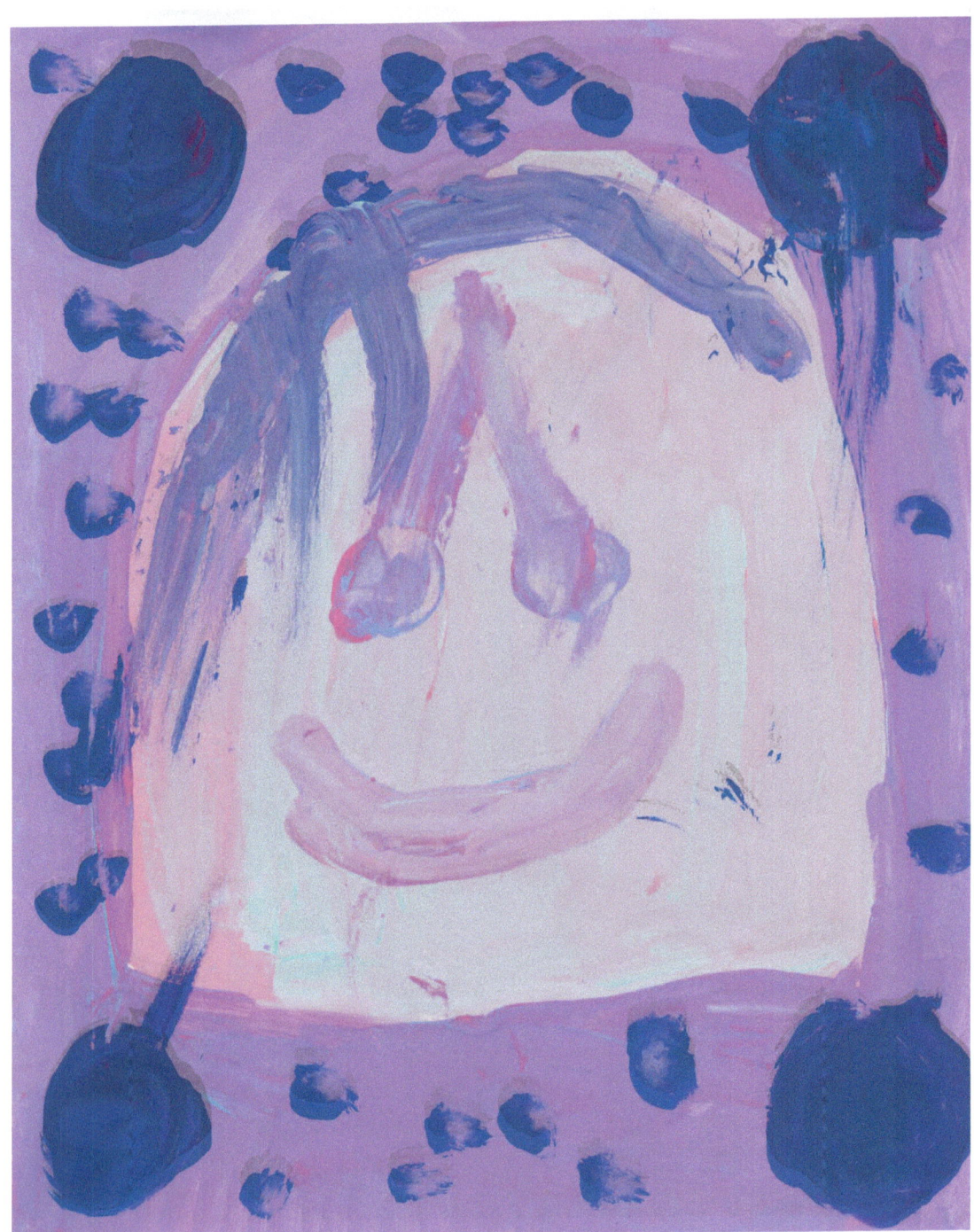

www.ingramcontent.com/pod-product-compliance
Lightning Source LLC
Chambersburg PA
CBHW051952210526
45473CB00023B/1059